URBAN LEGENDS

First Skyhorse Publishing edition 2018.

Skyhorse Publishing books may be purchased in bulk at special discounts for sales promotion, corporate gifts, fund-raising, or educational purposes. Special editions can also be created to specifications. For details, contact the Special Sales Department, Skyhorse Publishing, 307 West 36th Street, 11th Floor, New York, NY 10018 or info@skyhorsepublishing.com.

Skyhorse® and Skyhorse Publishing® are registered trademarks of Skyhorse Publishing, Inc.®, a Delaware corporation.

Visit our website at www.skyhorsepublishing.com.

10 9 8 7 6 5 4

Library of Congress Cataloging-in-Publication Data is available on file.

Cover design by Michael Short

Print ISBN: 978-1-5107-3315-2
E-Book ISBN: 978-1-5107-3318-3

Printed in the United States of America

URBAN LEGENDS

JAMES
PROUD

BIZARRE TALES YOU WON'T BELIEVE

Skyhorse Publishing

CONTENTS

CONTENTS

INTRODUCTION

Have you heard the one about the alligators that live in the sewers? What about the story of the woman who woke up in the middle of her own funeral? Is there really a black market trade in stolen body parts? From the unsettling to the downright scary, and from the totally unbelievable to the it-could-happen-to-you, everybody knows at least one urban legend. This is a collection of some of the most compelling from around the world.

Some of these stories are true, whereas others are pure fiction—and many are somewhere in between. What they all have in common is the power to capture the imagination and spread like wildfire. Many of the urban legends in this book go back decades and originally lived on thanks to word of mouth. The internet has given the tall tale a new lease of life: it all began with chain emails, followed by message boards, and now we have social media and viral videos. The nature of urban legends, both old and new, is to tap into common fears, stereotypes and prejudices, irrespective of where you come from. Strangers, crime, technology, clowns, children's dolls, travelling alone, dark nights...If it frightens people, it's probably in an urban legend—sometimes just the thrill of being freaked out is enough. Others are cautionary tales of stupidity with characters that need bringing down a peg or two, ending with a twist to keep the rest of us in line.

You might recognize stories that you'd always thought were true, but actually never happened, and others that you'd always assumed to be nonsense, but were actually based on real events. See if you can tell the truth from the fiction, and watch out for the twists...

SUPERNATURAL

CALLS FROM BEYOND

A middle-aged man was on a train to Los Angeles, on his way to a job interview. He had recently become engaged, and he hoped that the job would allow the pair to marry. At 4.30 p.m. the vehicle collided at 85 mph with a freight train running in the opposite direction, in one of the worst accidents in America's history.

His fiancée heard about the crash while driving to the train station with the man's parents and his siblings. Several of his loved ones received calls from the man's mobile phone so they naturally assumed that he had survived the accident, even though all they could hear when they picked up was static. Although their subsequent calls to him went straight to voicemail, all through the night they waited for confirmation that he had been found alive and well.

Twelve hours after the accident, having tracked the signal from his mobile phone, rescuers finally located him in the wreckage. He had died instantly in the crash...and yet 35 calls had been made from his phone—only to his nearest and dearest—as if the mobile had been reaching out to help lead them to his body.

MIDNIGHT FARE

A taxi driver working the night shift on a quiet Sunday was driving past a hospital. A young girl hailed him down and hurried into the car to get out of the rain. She was wearing a hood and her hair partly obscured her face. She requested that he take her to a lake nearby, which he thought was odd, but he reasoned that perhaps she lived near it. She didn't answer any of his questions, so he drove to the destination in silence, with the rain drumming on the car.

When they arrived, she asked him to wait for her, and she disappeared into the darkness. He waited for a long time, not wanting to abandon the girl out there on her own. Finally, she returned and asked to be taken to a new address, this time to a neighborhood that the driver knew. When they arrived, the girl got out of the car without paying the fare and disappeared inside a house. Annoyed, the driver got out of the taxi and knocked on the door. An elderly man opened it but there appeared to be no sign of the girl. When the driver asked about his mysterious passenger, the old man said that there were no children in the house, but then he explained something: he once had a daughter, but she had drowned in the lake in a car accident with her boyfriend many years earlier. He said that sometimes her spirit caught a cab to look for him in the lake, before returning to her childhood home. The old man asked, worried, "You didn't get a good look at her face, did you?" The driver replied he had not, and the old man smiled, "Good." He then paid the fare and closed the door. When the taxi driver got back to the car, he saw that in the place where the girl had sat down was a puddle of black water.

NURE-ONNA

Japanese children are often told the story of a keen swimmer who went for a dip every day in the lake near his house in the mountains. Usually, he was the only person there, as he swam early in the morning when the water was very cold. One day he thought he saw someone else in the lake but, as he approached the water, he realized that they weren't swimming—they were drowning. It was a young woman, waving her hands silently above the surface of the lake, so he dived right in and swam powerfully to her rescue. As he got closer, he saw the girl's long black hair swirling around her as she slipped beneath the choppy waters. He moved to grab her but suddenly his legs felt heavy and he could barely move his arms. He couldn't understand what was happening, but then he noticed something strange: the girl was no longer struggling but staring directly at him with black eyes. As he desperately tried to keep his head above water, he realized that instead of hands she had claws, and instead of legs she had the body of a great snake, which was wrapping itself around his torso and dragging him down into the depths. He was never seen again—being a hero can have its consequences...

CLACK CLACK

An American boy was sleeping over at a friend's house and they were both trying to outdo each other with telling scary stories. He'd seen all of his older brother's scary movies, so he wasn't that impressed with what he had heard so far. Then his friend's cousin turned up, heard what game they were playing and, despite their protestations, sat down and joined in.

He told them about a girl who was waiting for a train to her high school prom one night, when she saw a group of her friends on the other side of the tracks. Not wanting to be left out, she ran over a crossing just as the train was coming, and the wheels cut her in half at the waist. Ever since, people had reported seeing her legless ghost at the school, especially on prom night, when it was said that she would cut your body in half. And anybody who heard the story would see her in one month's time.

A few weeks later the boy was walking home from school, when a girl appeared over a wall and smiled at him. He smiled back and continued on his way when he heard a strange "clack clack" noise behind him. He looked around in horror: the girl was crawling over the wall, dragging herself on bony elbows. As she dropped to the floor, he saw that she had no legs and when she started crawling towards him, her elbows made the spine-chilling *clack clack* noise, as she gained on him. He didn't turn up to school the next day.

THE DOLL

For decades a small doll kept at a temple in Hokkaido prefecture, Japan, has captured the attention of Japanese people. The story goes that the doll, which has black hair and black eyes, and wears a traditional kimono, was the favorite of a little girl who died tragically young in the 1920s.

The girl carried the doll everywhere she went and, after her premature death, the family placed her favorite toy in an altar in her memory. The girl had cropped the doll's hair short to look like her own, and people would often comment that it looked suspiciously like its owner. Not long afterwards, the family noticed that the doll's hair appeared longer than it had been. Although they dismissed the notion as a figment of their imagination, eventually they couldn't ignore the fact that the hair was growing. When it reached the doll's knees, the family, suspecting some insensitive prank, cut the doll's hair so that it was short again but, of course, it only grew back longer. The family eventually placed the mysterious toy in a local temple, where it remains to this day. The monks at the temple cut the doll's hair on a regular basis and it always grows back. Many years after the doll arrived at the temple, the hair was tested and found to be that of a young child.

TUNNEL VISIONS

A busy highway in Tokyo, Japan, runs through a tunnel that lies underneath a very large and very old cemetery. The graveyard is not visible when driving a car underneath, but many drivers are said to have felt its presence over the years.

A man driving back from a late shift at work one night narrowly avoided hitting what he swore was a young mother with a small child, but after he managed to get his car under control and swerve to a stop, he saw that there was nobody there. His friends blamed lack of sleep, but he was sure there had been somebody standing in the middle of the road.

People in the know would say that he witnessed one of the sinister spirits emanating from the graveyard above and becoming trapped in the tunnel, stuck between this world and the afterlife. On more than one occasion drivers, usually male, have described how they glanced in their rear-view mirror and caught sight of a young girl with long black hair on the back seat, staring straight at them. If they managed to keep their car on the road and checked again, they would find that there was nothing there. Other reports include people hanging upside down or banging on car roofs, and mysterious handprints and faces appearing on windows. The area's taxi drivers are particularly wary: all of them know the stories of cabs being hailed by people in the tunnel, only for them to disappear when the door is opened.

HANAKO-SAN

Anybody who grew up in the West knows the legend of Bloody Mary, who will appear if you say her name three times into a mirror in a darkened room. The Japanese have their own version: you must go into an empty girls' bathroom and knock on the door of the last cubicle three times, then ask aloud, "Are you there Hanako-san?" When you open the door, you will see a young girl who was brutally murdered in a high school bathroom many years before. She always wears a red skirt.

BENJAMIN'S HOUSE

At the turn of the twentieth century, a wealthy family bought an old mansion in the south-west of England, high on the cliffs in a remote location, overlooking the sea. They lived with their young child, a boy named Ben, and several servants. Stories would reach the local villagers, who rarely saw the inhabitants of the house, that the owners were distant and cruel to their staff, who had little other choice of employment in the area. The devoutly religious lady of the house singled out one of the maids, a young cook, for particularly cruel treatment, claiming that the girl was evil and that she was corrupting the rest of the staff.

The maid would often return late from her weekends off, and the other servants liked to gossip: they said that she was a harlot, a liar and even a witch. She was a strong-minded girl and instead of denying the rumor, she played up to the stories told about her. When the boy's father found her performing strange rituals in the grounds of the house, she was beaten and dismissed. Before she left, she offered a doll to the boy, who had always liked her despite his parents' suspicions, as a peace offering. His parents were all for throwing it away, but the boy liked it—in fact, it became an instant favorite, and he even named it after himself: Benjamin.

He dressed the doll in clothes to match his own and would never let it out of his sight—or was it that he was never out of *its* sight? The boy would often talk to Benjamin in his room alone, even pretending to speak in its voice. His parents thought his behavior strange, but as he had no other friends to speak to and it kept him occupied, they let him be. Occasionally, the servants heard him arguing with the doll in his bedroom and one morning they heard him sobbing uncontrollably from behind a locked door. They told his father, who found the little boy hiding under the bed, because he said that Benjamin couldn't see him there. The father was again ready to get rid of the doll but the boy pleaded to let him keep it in the house.

A rumor started among the servants that the boy was not talking for the doll; the doll was talking for itself. It became common to hear loud noises coming from the boy's room at night, and when the door was opened, he would claim that Benjamin had done it. One of the maids reported being "followed" by the doll and spotting it at different upstairs windows, as if it were watching her work. It was said that the doll's face had a different expression depending on who was looking: sometimes happy, sometimes sad—sometimes angry.

The stories eventually caught the attention of a writer who was staying in the village and decided to investigate. He was rebuffed by the owners, who denied all knowledge, but he persevered. He managed to talk to some of the staff, who told him that the doll had a distinctive piercing laugh, which could be heard in the upper floors of the house, and was often spotted sitting in different rooms of the house when the boy wasn't at home; one servant even claimed to have seen it running across the hall. Eventually, the boy grew up, but he never left the house—and he never left Benjamin. When he died many years later, the household wasted no time in banishing the toy to the attic, where it was sometimes glimpsed peering out of the windows. The doll remained in exile upstairs for many years, until the house's new owners moved in. They had a little girl who one day, while roaming in the attic, discovered an old well-worn doll with a sad look on its face. Soon Benjamin was up to its old tricks: the girl appeared to be terrified of the doll, saying it had attacked her, but she couldn't bear to be parted from it. On one occasion, her older brother beheaded Benjamin with scissors and left it on the floor as a cruel sibling prank, only to find the doll the next day in his bedroom...with its head reattached and smiling.

THE HIGHGATE VAMPIRE

In the 1970s a London newspaper covered a juicy story that was terrifying the residents of a well-to-do suburb in the north of the city. The cast of characters included: a top-hatted gentleman

thought to be a vampire who had been sighted several times—
he apparently escaped from a cemetery each night to find fresh
victims—and a vampire hunter with a band of dedicated followers.
The paper reported that people walking in Highgate cemetery,
resting place of many famous individuals including Karl Marx, had
seen ghostly figures following them at night. A few days later it
emerged that graves in the cemetery had been disturbed and the
remains of a ritual act were found. Most disturbingly, an iron stake
had been driven through the lid of a coffin and into the corpse
inside.

The paper interviewed the self-proclaimed vampire hunter:
he claimed that whoever had placed the stake in the coffin was
mistaken and that the monster was still at large. Moreover, he
declared that he and his followers had stalked the vampire as he
was leaving the cemetery and that the creature was actually the
reanimated corpse of an eighteenth-century European gentleman:
he had been transported to London in a coffin after his death and
was now possessed by evil spirits. The hunter claimed that he had
tracked down the vampire to a great mausoleum in the cemetery,
where he had had the chance of putting a stake through his heart
as he was sleeping. However, he did not carry out the deed, as it
would have been illegal to desecrate a body in such a fashion, but
he took sensational photographs of the creature's evil, contorted
face and scattered garlic in the vault.

Then the body of a woman was found in the grounds of the
cemetery, not far from the mausoleum, causing a furore in the
media. Hundreds of people turned up at the cemetery night after
night in an attempt to find the vampire. The police had to guard
the place for several nights to put the locals' minds at rest. The
hunter eventually cornered the vampire in a nearby mansion,
where he had found refuge in a coffin. They performed an

exorcism, put a stake through the creature's heart and burned the corpse, thus ending the threat forever.

MODERN VAMPIRES

In Romania, land of the original Dracula, old habits die hard. Rumors of vampires rising from graves to prey on the living are still popular. In Transylvania in 2004, a group of villagers were worried about someone who had been recently buried. They thought he was responsible for a series of recent attacks in the community and decided to revert to ancient techniques in order to stop the crime spree. They went to the cemetery to dig up the body, which, they noticed, looked a lot fresher than would be expected, and a stake was driven through the heart. Then the organ was cut from the torso and burned, according to tradition. No more attacks were reported.

Vampire folklore has a long history in Romania, home as it was to the man who inspired Dracula: Vlad the Impaler, Prince of Wallachia in the fifteenth century. Vlad got his nickname because of his habit of impaling captured enemies on stakes. He carried out this practice with so many of his enemies that one visitor to the country described a "mighty forest" of corpses stuck on stakes that stunk to high heaven. When he complained to the Prince, it's said that the same visitor was "impaled high up, so that the smell of the others would not bother him."

It's not just in Eastern Europe that stories of vampires cause people to take drastic action. In rural nineteenth-century New England, an outbreak of tuberculosis took hold, killing many, and as the disease tended to kill several members of the same family, worried locals surmised that the dead were taking others down with them. In order to try to arrest the outbreak, they invoked ancient rituals designed to stop vampires. In 1892 the Brown family of Exeter, Rhode Island, were hit by the disease. A young girl, Mercy, died, and her mother followed soon afterwards. As inevitably happened with the disease, Mercy's brother also fell ill. The family felt that their only option was to exhume and examine the bodies. The father enlisted the help of villagers for the job; they found that Mercy, who had died two months previously, looked suspiciously lifelike and that her heart contained fresh blood. This was a sure sign that she was the vampire to blame for the deaths, so her heart was cut out and ritually burned. The ashes were given to her brother on his sickbed, while others inhaled the smoke in a belief that it would protect them. Unsurprisingly, neither method worked.

THE SCHOOL BUS

Several decades ago, an odd story appeared in a local newspaper in a rural region of Wales. On the last day of term, a school bus taking children home was making its usual crossing over a railway line that ran up a mountain. The driver never liked taking the children over the crossing, but he had done it hundreds of times without incident. However, this time something went wrong, and the bus stopped right in the middle of the tracks. As the driver frantically tried to restart the engine, his worst nightmare began to come true: he heard a train sound its horn in the distance. Within seconds a heavy goods vehicle was looming large in the window. His first instinct was to save the children, so he leapt from the bus and smashed open the emergency exit. The last thing he heard was the terrible noise as the locomotive's brakes screeched in vain and the children screamed as they jumped off the bus. The last thing he saw was the train driver above him, shielding his eyes as he awaited the inevitable. The train obliterated the bus, but by some miracle only the bus driver lost his life.

Over time the small mining community slowly forgot about the accident, until a recent story appeared in the same paper. It reported that an elderly man, a retired teacher, was driving over the same railway crossing when his car stalled on the tracks. The alarm began to sound and his panic grew as he fumbled with his seat belt. Just as he opened the door, and the guard rails lowered behind him, he felt the car shift, as though it was being lifted up from underneath, and the next thing he knew the train was thundering past behind him, so close that it rocked the car. He was so shaken that he had to get out of his vehicle and call his wife to drive him home, which is when he checked the back of his car for damage: the train had missed it by a foot. It was also at that moment that he noticed the marks on the boot of his car: they were bloody handprints. The man looked around in a panic, but there was no one else in sight.

RED PAPER

Japanese children scare each other by repeating the tale of what happened to two schoolboys many years ago. One day one of the boys went to the bathroom, only to find that there was no toilet paper in the stall. As he cursed to himself, he heard a voice asking him whether he wanted red or blue paper. He answered "red" and all the blood seeped out of his body so that he died in minutes. The story spread around the school. Some months later the boy's friend found himself in the same toilet stall, and again there was no paper. He heard the same voice ask him what paper he would like. Knowing the story and remembering what had happened to his friend, he chose blue. Gradually, his throat began to tighten and soon he was struggling to breathe. Classmates found him dead, blue in the face from suffocation.

THE SURVIVOR

One sunny summer day, a young couple were driving down to the coast for a vacation. They had left the town and were winding through the hills when they noticed a woman at the side of the road, flagging them down. She looked distressed and her clothes were covered in blood, so they quickly pulled over and asked her what had happened. She struggled to get her words out; she appeared to have an injury to her neck and was in pain. They finally established that she and her family had been in a car crash, although there was no vehicle visible from the road. The woman pointed over the side of the valley, saying that the car was somewhere down there and her husband was dead, but her baby was trapped in the back seat and he was still alive when she left him.

The man started to clamber down the valley through broken trees, while his girlfriend said she would call for help and look after the woman. He saw that the car had rolled a long way down the hill, and looked in a very bad way, but as he got closer he could hear the muffled sounds of a young child. The wreckage was terrible and he could barely see the driver. Although the back door was bent into the frame, he tugged with all his might and managed to wrench it open. He was able to pull the screaming baby out and carry him back up the hill.

As he hurried back to his girlfriend, he noticed that the woman was no longer with her. "Where did she go?" he asked.

"She went to see her baby. I tried to stop her," replied his girlfriend.

So the man handed the baby over and returned to the crash site to find the boy's mother. As there was no sign of her, he checked the rest of the vehicle. He hauled the smashed windscreen out of the way and saw that the driver was clearly beyond help, so he turned his attention to the passenger and what he saw took his breath away: it was the mother who had flagged them down, clearly dead and trapped in the wreckage all that time.

ESMERALDA

Around 100 years ago, a sensational story filled the papers in Nottingham, England. A young gypsy girl named Esmeralda, who was visiting the area with her family, was raped one night and the attacker was never found. It was said that the police weren't bothered about the fate of a traveller. What the papers didn't know was that she had fallen pregnant after the attack and gave birth to a child, but he was horribly deformed and didn't survive his first year. He was buried in an unmarked grave in a field on the borders of the city. Esmeralda was said to have visited the place every time she came through the area with her family until she was middle aged. On one occasion she found that the grave had been dug up, the coffin opened and the body taken. After struggling to deal with the memories of her ordeal for many years, the shock of that discovery tipped her over the edge and she lost her mind. Esmeralda was shunned by her community and ended her days in a cruel asylum in the city.

The story was forgotten, and the field became a children's playground after the war. For many years locals had reported strange happenings at the site: some described the sounds of a baby crying, or something like the shrieks of a fox or a feral cat. Children playing would find the mutilated remains of animals, such as birds, cats and once even a large dog. A newspaper report warned parents that a young girl had been approached by an old woman wearing strange clothes who had asked if she had seen her child and then had muttered a curse when the girl ran off.

One night in the 1960s, a man was walking his dog, a German shepherd, through the park. The dog was running off the leash when his owner heard him growling somewhere in the darkness. He called for him, scared that he might bite a stranger, but then came a terrible yowling, and the animal raced back to his side, whimpering. It had a vicious gash on its nose and was limping. Then the man heard something wailing from the trees, like nothing he had heard before, and caught sight of something moving quickly across the ground towards him. He didn't wait to see what it was and ran home as fast as he could.

THE WOMAN IN WHITE

A group of children were playing in a river in their hometown near Mexico City—a place they usually visited to let off steam. A woman appeared and started to ask them questions. She stood out from the locals because of her appearance: she was dressed all in white and immaculately groomed. She spoke quietly and occasionally sobbed, asking the children if they had seen Marcus and Gabriela, whom she called her "little babies." One of the boys was called Marcus, but he didn't know the lady, so they ignored her.

The woman disappeared as quietly as she had appeared.

When the time came to leave the river, the children noticed that Marcus was missing. They assumed that he had gone home by himself and thought nothing of it, but by the next morning he hadn't turned up and the whole town was looking for him. He was eventually found face down in the river; he had drowned. His family assumed he had got into trouble while swimming with the others, until one of the children told her mother about the woman in white and how she had been looking for her children. When Marcus's mother heard the tale, her blood ran cold; she knew who had taken her son. Three more children from the town disappeared over the following month, and each death was preceded by a sighting of the pale-faced woman in white, asking after her children.

Centuries earlier, when the Spanish invaded South America, a beautiful native interpreter became involved with one of the commanders and had two children by him. The man eventually married a Spanish woman, shunning his native mistress and their offspring. In her grief she went mad and drowned the children in the river before leaping off a bridge herself. She tried to enter heaven, but could not gain access without her children, so she was condemned to roam the earth, trapped between the living and the dead. The legend goes that she wanders the land looking for her children, taking any she finds that resemble her own and drowning them, in order to bring them to heaven to try to receive forgiveness for her terrible crimes.

LA MALA HORA

Maria from Arizona received a phone call from her best friend, Rosanna, who sounded distraught. Rosanna was breaking up with her boyfriend and he had left the house in a rage, so she asked if her friend could come and keep her company. As Maria's husband was away on a business trip, she was feeling lonely so she decided to accept. It was late, just after midnight, when she left her house in her car, and the dark roads were deserted. She couldn't escape the feeling that something was watching or following her, but she told herself that it was just her mind playing tricks.

Halfway to her destination, she stopped at a crossroads and suddenly a dark shape, like a cloud of smoke, rolled towards her car. Then it disappeared. The lights turned green and she accelerated but immediately slammed on the brakes when she saw a figure in the road right in front of her. She was small, like a girl, but with the face of an old lady twisted into a hateful grin. Her eyes glowed red, and she bared black and sharpened teeth. She crawled on top of the car, and started to scrape and hit the window on the driver's side with clawed hands. Maria put her foot to the floor in sheer terror and the car lurched away from the crossroads, leaving her attacker on the tarmac. As she sped away from the lights, she realized with horror that the demon woman was still chasing her car and somehow keeping pace, her talons scraping at the metal with a terrible noise. She accelerated to well over the speed limit, her heart pounding, and then the noise stopped. Her heart was hammering in her chest as she watched in her rear-view mirror the figure in the middle of the road: she was standing still but seemed to be as close as before; she was growing towards the sky and her great claws were so large that they touched the ground. Then the car turned a corner and she was gone.

When Maria reached Rosanna's house, she screeched to a halt, ran up the drive and slammed her fists on the door, shouting to be let in. Her friend opened the door in fright, and Maria told her to shut it and lock it. She closed all the curtains and told Rosanna not to look out of the window.

"What happened?" Rosanna asked, and Maria explained what she had seen on the road: the dark shape, the woman with claws and how she seemed to grow in the moonlight behind her. Her friend listened quietly, kept looking at her watch and seemed to know what she was talking about.

"Are you sure you were stopped at a crossroads?"

"Yes, I'm sure," replied Maria, listening carefully for any noises coming from outside.

"It may have been *la mala hora*," explained Rosanna. "It means "the evil hour". They say she appears at a crossroads when someone is about to die. If you manage to escape her grasp, someone you love will die in your place."

Maria was horrified, but she tried to make light of it, saying that she must have imagined the whole thing. However, she knew that she hadn't, and she couldn't stop shaking.

It took her hours to get to sleep, but when she awoke the following morning, she wondered if it had all been a dream. Rosanna didn't mention anything over breakfast and Maria slowly forgot about it. Later that day, as she was driving home, her phone kept ringing but she didn't stop to answer it. She had to pass over the same crossroads on her journey back but was relieved to find that in the daylight she wasn't frightened. When she reached home, she saw a police car waiting in her driveway and wondered whether she had been burgled—or maybe her husband had been caught speeding again?

The officers got out of the car but wouldn't tell her anything until she went inside. They asked if she was alone in the house and said that her husband had been found dead in his hotel. They thought that he had been followed back to his room by a thief, who had forced his way in and stabbed him to death for his wallet. Maria didn't want to believe them, as she had spoken to him late the night before, so she asked what time it had happened. "Not long after midnight," came the reply.

THE PSYCHIC

A girl and some friends went to a show put on by a "psychic medium" at a local theater. They didn't know if they really believed in those sorts of things, but they thought it might be fun. Who knew, they might even get an insight into their future! One of their friends had been to see the same psychic for a private tarot card reading, and been told that she would find the man of her dreams and marry him within six months. As that's exactly what then happened, maybe there was something to it after all!

It was a fun evening, if a little creepy at times, as the psychic seemed to be aware of things that only they and their loved ones knew. The psychic did a reading of the cards for the girl's friends, writing something inside an envelope for each of them, and said that they could open them straight away or later at home. They all tore them open and read out predictions about marriage, heartache and great wealth.

Then the psychic asked the girl to come up to the stage and laid out the cards. She looked at her with a pained look on her face and claimed that something was stopping her from seeing clearly—had she lost a loved one recently? The girl replied honestly that she hadn't. The psychic asked to read her palm instead and traced the lines on her skin, nodding solemnly. "I can see your future now, my dear; it's all very clear." She laid down her hand and handed her an envelope that she already had in her pocket. Her friends begged her to open it, but the girl pretended not to be too bothered by the whole affair, saying that she would leave it until she got home.

Once the evening ended, the girl bid farewell to her friends and drove home alone. She had pulled out onto a main road and was looking at the envelope lying on the passenger seat, thinking about what might be written inside, when she was startled by the blast of a horn and flashing of lights. A large lorry had missed the back of her car by inches as she pulled out in front. She breathed a sigh of relief and drove on nervously.

Eventually, she couldn't resist the temptation any longer and leaned over to pick up the envelope. As she did so, the car drifted slightly over the white dividing lines of the road, just enough for a car coming from the opposite direction to smash into hers and shove it violently into the path of the following truck. She was killed instantly. When the firefighters arrived to cut her body out of the wreckage, they found a bloodied envelope on the floor. It made its way to her family, who decided to open it. The card inside said, "You have no future."

COW HEAD

A teacher in China was travelling with his students on a school trip in the mountains above the town where they lived. It was a long journey and the students, who had grown bored and restless, started to play up, so the teacher suggested that they should tell each other stories. He joined in and told them several spooky tales that soon kept them quiet as the night drew in. Then the bus driver asked him if he'd ever heard of a very old story known only as "cow head."

The teacher looked shocked and went quiet for a moment. He told the driver that he had heard of the story but didn't know how it ended. Besides, he had heard that it was too frightening for children. Some said that people who had merely listened to the tale had lost their minds, and there were even rumors that it had taken lives. The bus driver smiled to himself, but the children overheard their conversation and were soon clamoring to hear the "cow head" story.

The teacher reasoned that he couldn't do any real harm, as he didn't know the whole story anyway; he could make it up as he went along. He started to tell the tale of a government official who had arrived to take a census in a remote village in the mountains, many decades ago. The last census had suggested that there should have been several hundred citizens there, but the place was completely deserted. The only signs of life were the bones of animals scattered in the dust. The official found the place unnerving and travelled to the next settlement, a long way over a mountain pass, where he asked what had happened to the villagers. They said that nobody knew for sure, but there were rumors that they went mad and ate each other during a terrible famine.

The official called in colleagues from the government to investigate. Amongst the animal skeletons, they found the strange remains of a man with what appeared to be the head of a cow. Locals said that the man had seemed perfectly normal when he first arrived in the village, but he had brought a terrible curse down upon them.

At this point in the narration, the children on the bus started to cry and asked the teacher to stop telling the story. But something had come over him: he was no longer in control and he continued with the tale as though in a trance, staring dead ahead. The children were trying to cover their ears and some started to foam at the mouth. They attempted to move from their seats but their arms were pinned down by their sides. The teacher continued to recite the story with a blank look in his eyes, a tale that became more horrific with every word. The last thing the children remembered before they passed out was the look in their teacher's eyes.

When a passing driver came upon the bus many hours later, the teacher and all the students were still unconscious. It took days for them to come round but the teacher was found to be in a deep coma from which he never recovered. The bus driver was never seen again. None of the children on the bus who heard the cow head tale would ever dare to recite it, not even to each other.

PRIME REAL ESTATE

A large, pretty family house in Amityville, New York, has a secret and that's why it has remained empty for decades, despite a local property boom. In 1974 a man murdered his entire family in that house, shooting his wife and three small children with a hunting rifle as they slept. At his trial the defense tried to get him declared insane, as he claimed that he was being controlled by strange voices in his head belonging to the previous occupants of the house, who had told him to commit the crime.

The experts, however, did not agree that he was mad. The jury convicted him of first-degree murder and he was given four consecutive life sentences, one for each life he had taken. The house lay empty for a year, as the family's relatives couldn't bear to even set foot in the place. They finally sold it way under market price to a young family from out of town, who had never heard about the murders. When neighbors finally told them, they pretended that they weren't bothered, but certain things started to make sense, as they had been plagued with problems since moving in: the water ran red from the taps and mysterious foul-smelling black gunk oozed from the toilets. The father found strange marks in the door frames, which looked to him like the imprint of a small child's teeth, but his own children denied any knowledge.

Each of the family members reported hearing the sound of music at night, from an unknown source, and, strangest of all, their youngest daughter became obsessed with a demonic imaginary friend that she described as a pig. The parents didn't believe in ghosts, or anything supernatural, but the kids refused to go upstairs at night, so they called in a priest to perform an exorcism. They told themselves it was just to reassure the kids that the house was safe. The priest was relaxed and friendly when he arrived, but he became noticeably disturbed after blessing the upstairs rooms and left before performing a full exorcism. He told them that although the house was not haunted, on no account should anyone sleep in the third bedroom. They were sceptical, but they locked that door. The happenings continued, but the family were too proud to move—who would buy the place anyway? The final straw came when the young mother was woken by dark red liquid dripping from the ceiling of the bedroom, and the family moved out to a motel that very night. They had lasted six weeks. Nobody in the neighborhood was surprised; some had even commented on how the new owner looked remarkably similar to the murderer and joked darkly that he had escaped just in time to save his family.

LAKE RONKONKOMA

Lake Ronkonkoma, in New York State, is an ancient and extremely deep lake that has been linked to many tragic stories. It's often claimed that someone has drowned there every year as far back as records began.

There was once a tribe of Native Americans living on the shores of the lake, at the mouth of a river, and a rival tribe was based on the opposite side. The princess of one tribe fell in love with the prince from the other, and once the elders found out, she was forbidden to even cross the river, never mind see her prince again. The two tribes had been warring for decades, and there was too much bad blood between them to risk a union.

Young love being what it is, the prince and princess took a dugout canoe one night and escaped onto the lake. They didn't have a plan, but they wanted to be together. They had not been paddling for long when the wind suddenly grew into a monstrous storm, and the surface of the lake was whipped into great waves. They held onto the canoe for dear life as the water around them surged into a foaming whirlpool, and they were dragged down to the bottom of the lake in a tragic embrace. Afterwards, the elders told the youths of both tribes about the pair, explaining that the lake spirits did not agree with the union and that was why they had taken those young lives.

Despite the stories associated with it, the beautiful lake still draws young people to its shores every summer. They paddle boats out into the middle and dare each other to dive into the cool waters. Every year someone fails to surface—always someone who is in a loving relationship—and the body is never recovered. The story goes that they are cursed by the tragic Native American princess, who, jealous of her victim's happiness, drags them down into the depths.

THE BLACK LADY OF THE WOODS

A local newspaper in Lincolnshire, England, published images taken by a girl who had been walking with her cousin in woods near her home. She told the paper that they had been playing around with her camera in the dark, taking pictures of her cousin, who was an aspiring model, and didn't see anybody else around. But when the girls looked at the photographs a couple of days later on a computer, they saw that they had captured strange shadows in the trees: the floating figures of mysterious people and ghostly faces in the darkness. The girls didn't really believe in ghosts, but after a little research on the history of the woods, they knew exactly what they had captured: the Black Lady of the Woods.

Hidden in the undergrowth is an abandoned stone cottage near a pond where, in the seventeenth century, a poor gamekeeper lived with his wife and son, or so the story goes. After the outbreak of the English Civil War he was forced into fighting for his master, who supported the king, and marched off to battle. He told his wife that he would return within six months, but he never did, and she took to wandering the woods to look for him.

One Christmas, a band of Roundheads fighting the king rode through the forest on horseback. Identifying the land as enemy territory, they claimed the wood and everything in it, including the gamekeeper's cottage. They stole everything the wife had, including her young son, and burned the house. It was said that the woman died of grief and, from that day on, people have claimed to see a lady—hunched over and crying, dressed in a black cloak and hood—wandering the woods, looking for her missing husband and child. It's believed that she can still be seen in the forest to this day, and if you walk in the woods at Christmas time and utter the words, "Black lady, black lady, I've stolen your baby" three times, she will appear in front of you.

BETSY'S VOICE

Boy Scouts on camping trips tell their rookie recruits a story that dates back to the early days of scouting after World War Two.

In a forest surrounding an abandoned airfield, there was an old house where Scouts would play hide-and-seek. The place had been bought cheaply by a young couple, Betsy and her husband Johnny, before the war. They hoped to renovate it and make it their perfect family home. Betsy was an aspiring singer whose career was cut short by the outbreak of the war. She was driving down the track from the house one night, when a truck full of soldiers coming back from the pub came the other way. They were making a racket, completely inebriated, and distracting the driver. He took his eyes off the road for a moment to tell them to pipe down, just long enough to veer into Betsy's path, crashing head first into her car and killing her instantly. Her body was so badly disfigured that the police wouldn't let her husband, Johnny, say goodbye to her. She was identified only by the large diamond ring he had given her, a family heirloom. Johnny buried the ring with her, devastated, and moved to another country, letting the house go to ruin.

Many years later the house was discovered by a group of Scouts on a hike through the forest from their camp. It seemed like the perfect place to light a campfire, play games and tell creepy stories. But it was not to be an idyllic Boy Scout adventure. The first thing they noticed was a female voice joining them in songs around the fire, which was odd because back then girls weren't allowed in the Scouts. Above the crackling of the flames, they heard her again, and it sounded as if she was inside the house. Finally, they saw her, initially looking out of the windows and then walking round the campfire: a terribly disfigured girl in a pretty dress. And then Betsy was gone.

The next morning one of the boys could not be woken. His mates were horrified to discover that he was dead, and the only signs of any injuries suffered were some nasty scratches on his face. "Betsy did it!" cried one of the boys, when he saw the body and, after some coaxing, he recounted what had happened in the night.

Betsy had returned to pay the lads a visit in the small hours and woken two of the boys with her singing. She asked them one by one if they thought she had a beautiful voice. The first boy had been too scared to answer and an angry Betsy slashed him across the face with her diamond ring, saying that once he fell asleep, he would never wake up again. Then she asked the other boy the same question and, without hesitation, he told her that she did indeed have a beautiful voice, so Betsy smiled and disappeared into the woods, singing all the way. The terrified boys tried to stay awake, but eventually they both fell asleep. Only one of them awoke in the morning. To this day Scouts are told to listen out for Betsy around the campfire and tell her what she wants to hear; she always wanted to be a singer, but she never liked critics.

MILK BOTTLES

Two old men ran a general store in a small town in the American Midwest. The Depression had hit and business was hard: the customers stopped visiting and soon only a few regulars were keeping them afloat. One day a young woman dressed all in white entered the store, carrying an empty milk bottle. She placed it on the counter and one of the men filled it with milk from the churn, asking for ten cents in return. The girl, who had a sad look in her eyes, did not reply; instead, she picked up the bottle and quietly left the store. The man was too surprised to say anything and when he followed her out of the shop, she was nowhere to be found. He went back inside, muttering to himself that she was probably a migrant from the city who didn't know how things worked out there.

He told his partner what had happened and to watch out for her. The next day she returned, again carrying an empty milk bottle. This time he told her that he knew that times were hard, but she had to pay like everybody else. He filled the bottle from the churn, but again she ignored him and walked out with the milk. On this occasion, however, the two men were ready, and they followed her through the town. She moved quickly, and they could barely keep up, but they saw that she headed for the church and stopped in front of a gravestone, where she disappeared. The two men couldn't believe their eyes, but they figured they couldn't both be seeing things. Then they heard the sound of a baby crying close by, but they couldn't see anybody. They realized that the noise was coming directly from the gravestone where the woman had vanished into thin air. They returned with shovels from their store, informing the sheriff on their way, and as they dug into the grave, the crying got louder. When they lifted the coffin out, they found a live baby inside, next to the woman from the store, who was clearly dead, and two empty milk bottles.

SCARY STORIES

BACKSEAT DRIVER

One summer night, a British driver was forced to pull into a deserted petrol station—the only one around. She was in a hurry and didn't want to hang around any longer than was necessary, so she proceeded to pay at the pump and started to fill up her car. Suddenly, a man's voice came over the loudspeaker, telling her to come into the garage to pay. She pretended she hadn't heard him and continued to fill the tank. He spoke again and told her that there was a problem with her credit card so she would have to pay in the kiosk. Then the pump stopped.

Now she was annoyed—she was sure that there was nothing wrong with her card, but she didn't want to drive off without paying, so she walked over to the garage, where the man beckoned her inside. She angrily protested that her card worked perfectly well and that she had places to be, but he interrupted her and locked the door. He quietly told her that he had watched a man sneak into her car when she was distracted at the pump, and he had already called the police. The woman looked out of the window: she saw the back door of her car wide open and a hooded figure walking quickly away from the station.

DATE NIGHT

One summer evening a teenage girl who lived in a remote English village was picked up by a boy for their second date. They were driving through the countryside when he mentioned that they were running out of petrol and therefore might not make it home. She thought he was joking, but she didn't find it particularly funny, especially when the car spluttered to a halt under an old oak tree—they really had run out of fuel. They both glanced at their mobile phones but neither could get a signal in such an isolated spot.

"Maybe we'll just have to stay here until morning?" he suggested. This didn't go down well with his date, so he told her to stay in the car and lock the doors while he went looking for help: the village was only a few miles back the other way and there was an old-fashioned phone box there if his phone still didn't work. The girl was understandably angry at her useless date for managing to run out of fuel and leaving her stranded in the middle of nowhere, but she settled down to wait for his return. It was too quiet for her liking, with the only sound being the wind, so she turned on the radio to keep her company. A news bulletin was being read out, but the reception was terrible so she put on a CD instead.

An hour passed, then two, and she started to get worried, wondering if he had abandoned her. Maybe he had been hit by a car on the dark country roads? She had heard of such accidents happening before. Then the car battery died and the music stopped. She cursed and slammed the dashboard. Suddenly, she heard a thump, followed by a scratching or tapping sound on the roof of the car. She told herself that it was probably a tree branch—it was a windy night—but it was a loud noise, so she kept still and didn't make a sound. The noises continued and her imagination began to play tricks on her—was someone out there? Her fear continued to grow, but she didn't dare open the door to escape. Just when she couldn't bear it any longer, flashing blue lights lit up the car and she breathed a sigh of relief, thinking that her date must have come back with some help. The car stopped and a policeman walked slowly towards her, but there was no sign of the boy. The officer shined his torch through the window and beckoned her out of the car.

"You're safe, but keep your eyes down and don't look back at the car," he instructed.

Confused, the girl asked if the policeman had seen her date. "There's time for that later," came the reply. She opened the police car door but could not resist a quick look back. What she saw made her freeze in terror: the boy was hanging upside down from the oak tree, lit by the flashing lights and swaying in the wind. His bloodied head was knocking on the car and his fingernails scraping the roof. "Didn't you listen to the radio?" asked the policeman. "A murderer just escaped from the mental hospital in town."

DON'T TURN ON THE LIGHT

Student halls of residence are strange places: you never know who or what you might find in your room. You don't really know the people you're suddenly living with, but everybody wants to make friends—they're always inviting themselves around and there's no real privacy. One Friday night at a university in England, first-year student Jennie was getting excited about a freshers' event that was taking place that evening. She was trying to persuade Emily, her new roommate, to come along, but the latter didn't feel like partying, so eventually Jennie left her there and went to the party alone. Later that evening, she came back to the room to get something, leaving the light off so as not to wake Emily, before returning to the event. When Jennie awoke late the next morning, she didn't remember much about getting home. As she rolled out of bed, she saw that Emily also appeared to be still asleep, which wasn't like her at all. Then she saw the blood on the sheets: Emily was dead, her throat cut. Above her, on the wall and scrawled in blood, were the words, "Aren't you glad you didn't turn on the light?"

THE RED ROOM

You are browsing on your computer one evening. You are supposed to be working on a project but instead are trawling through social media posts. Suddenly, a pop-up window appears with a cryptic question: "Do you like...?" You assume it's an advert and close the window. You try to get back to what you were doing, but the same question keeps popping up. Then you hear a child's voice saying, "Do you like...?" Thinking it must be some kind of computer virus, and as the voice becomes more and more insistent and aggressive, you try to ignore it. Then the screen turns red and the same window pops up again, but this time it asks, "Do you like the red room?"

Then you remember that you've heard of this happening to other people, and the memory makes your blood run cold. A list of names appears on the screen—a list of victims, all of whom were found in a room painted red with their own blood. You're scared, but you can't help clicking through it. The last name is yours, and you hear a noise behind you...

FEAR OF NEEDLES

A series of mysterious and frightening events were reported to police forces in cities across the United States in the early 1990s. In one such incident, a man in Seattle reported to a local hospital in a panic, complaining of a small puncture wound to his right arm. He explained that he had been outside a bar in the city when he felt a sharp pain in his shoulder, as a young woman in noticeably poor health brushed past him. She was carrying a sharp implement, possibly a surgical needle, and she hissed, "Welcome to the HIV club," while looking him directly in the eye. He frantically removed his shirt and saw the puncture wound. When he recovered from the shock to look for the perpetrator, she was nowhere to be found. He went to the police a few days later, but despite trawling through surveillance camera footage of the busy street, they could not track the woman down.

HOOKED

Young people in Colorado know the story of the hardened hitman who lost his mind after he was hired to kill an entire family. The job went wrong, and the contract killer lost both his hands in a gangland punishment. He was subsequently incarcerated at a secure mental hospital out of town and told that he would never be released. In place of his hands the prison authorities attached two large hooks. Several years went by and people had forgotten about him, until one night he escaped after murdering a guard who had taken pity on him.

Bulletins went out on the local radio all night: he was highly dangerous and should not be approached. A young couple who had driven into the country for some privacy heard the reports while they were parked in a popular location overlooking the town. They realized that they had driven past the psychiatric facility only a few minutes earlier. The girl didn't want to be out at night when the killer was on the loose, but the boy told her it would be fine and that they had probably caught him by then anyway. However, his date was having none of it so the boy reluctantly fired up the car and drove back into town, listening to the radio for updates. All the way home they heard a knocking noise coming from somewhere on the car, which he explained away as a regular problem. When they reached her house and got out of the vehicle, they saw what had been causing the noise: a large hook was hanging on the passenger door handle, covered in blood.

BEHIND THE MASK

A child in Japan was walking home from school one evening. The friends who usually walked with her had already gone home, but she was only one street away from her house. She saw a young woman walking towards her, wearing a surgical mask like those that many Japanese people use to protect themselves from smog and diseases. She stopped in front of the child and leaned down towards her. The child was not worried, as she seemed friendly enough.

"Where are you going?" the woman asked.

"I'm going home from school; my house is just down the road there."

"Do you think I'm beautiful?" came the unexpected question. The girl politely, if a little concerned, said yes.

The woman then asked, as she removed the mask, "How about now?" and revealed a horrific wound that slashed her mouth from ear to ear.

She bent down to the frightened girl and asked again through her mutilated lips, "How about now?" The girl was horrified by her appearance but she had been brought up to be always polite, so she told her that she still looked beautiful. Then the terrifying figure disappeared.

The next day at school the girl told her friends what she had seen and they immediately recognized the story. They told her that the woman had appeared to many girls over the years, but not all of them had been so lucky. If she hadn't said the right thing, the woman would have cut the same terrible smile into the girl's own face with a pair of scissors and condemned her to roam the streets in a mask. The shocked girl did not walk home alone again for a very long time.

THE GREEN MAN

In Pittsburgh children are told the tale of the Green Man: a terrifying figure who lives alone in an abandoned house and wanders the country lanes at night, looking for kids to chase. He was also known as Charlie No-Face, because he had a terrible disfigurement; some said that he was born that way, whereas others believed that he was struck by lightning. Other possible explanations included an accident involving power lines or a horrendous crime that drove him insane. Whatever the cause, it had made his skin glow green in the dark, and just viewing his face was enough to induce terror. However, you always had plenty of warning before you came across him, as he was blind, so you could hear him tapping his way along the road with his stick.

Kids who played in the country at night would scare each other with stories about him, and young couples who drove out to the "Green Man Tunnel" under the railroad would keep an eye out for him, as everybody knew that Charlie No-Face liked to wait under the bridge and tap on the steamy windows of cars with his stick. If you were brave, you would drive round the roads where he had been seen before, trying to catch sight of his face. Cars would drive from miles around.

Tragically, there was a real person behind this myth, but he wasn't called Charlie. He was a local boy who had suffered a near-fatal electric shock aged eight, after daring to climb up a railway bridge. In doing so he accidentally touched a live electrical wire and was blasted with 20,000 volts. He lost his left arm below the elbow, as well as his eyes and nose, and his face was severely burned. Somehow he survived and eventually returned home to his family. He lived into old age, mostly spending his days inside, as his appearance in the bright light of day would scare people, but he wandered the country lanes at night, looking for someone to talk to. Once people got over his shocking appearance and got to know him, they said that he was actually a nice guy—proof of the saying that you shouldn't judge a book by its cover.

CLOWNING AROUND

A couple went out for a dinner date one night and left their children with a new babysitter. The mother was a little unsure about her, as she was quite young, and the children hadn't been sleeping well lately after scaring each other with stories about a bogeyman hiding in their bedrooms. She wanted to ring to check how things were going at home, but the father reassured her that it was better not to interfere. Just then the mother's mobile phone rang and it was the babysitter, who said that there was no problem—the kids were fine—but "the clown" was creeping out all of them. Would it be OK if she moved it?

"What clown?" the mother asked.

"That weird clown figure that is standing in the corner of the living room?" the sitter explained. The mother told her to grab the children, go next door immediately and call her as soon as they got there. The babysitter replied, "OK, but why? There's nothing to worry about."

The mother replied, "There is something to worry about. We don't own a clown statue."

DON'T LOOK BEHIND YOU

A young woman was driving home in her new SUV one night from a 24-hour supermarket. The high driving position made her feel safer on the road after her last car, a hatchback, was written off in an accident with a truck. A few minutes after she had pulled onto a main road, she noticed bright lights in her rear-view mirror. She paid no attention to them but they continued to dazzle her: the large truck behind her was flashing his lights. She decided to ignore the driver and accelerated away from him. It wasn't safe to stop and she wasn't far from her home in the suburbs, where her boyfriend would be waiting. Then the truck loomed in her mirror again and she could see the driver trying to get her to pull over. She was worried he was going to ram her off the road, but soon she reached her junction and pulled off the main road. To her horror, however, she saw that the truck was still following her, so she put her foot down and screeched to a halt outside her house, running for the door. The truck driver pulled up some way behind her, lowered his window and yelled, "Get in your house and lock the door!" She turned round in surprise, as her boyfriend opened the door, and saw in the truck's headlights a man roll out from underneath her car and run off down the road. When he had gone, the truck driver got out of his cab and approached her, explaining why he had been following her since she had left the supermarket: "That guy has been hanging underneath your car all the way here. I think he had a knife."

BLACK-EYED TEENS

This story first appeared in the early days of the internet, posted on a message board. A young professional in a Midwestern American town had gone to pick up some supplies from a late-night convenience store. After leaving the shop, he got into his car and prepared to drive off, when he heard a knock at the window. Standing there were two small boys, both quite young and wearing hoods. He wound the window down to see what they wanted and instantly felt that something was not quite right with these children, who were asking him where he lived. He wasn't exactly scared, but for some reason he lied and said that he lived on the opposite side of town. They told him that was where they lived as well and that they needed a lift home because they had missed their bus. At that point it was past 10 p.m. and the man was aware that the buses had stopped running a few hours previously: what were they doing out at this time on their own?

The boys asked if he was going to let them in, saying that they were getting hungry, and one of them put his hand on the door handle, which the man quickly locked from the inside. The taller of the pair said that they were only kids, insisting, "We're not going to do anything bad, but we can't get in the car unless you ask us." This kind of talk alarmed the driver. He started the car, but they knocked again, and he wondered whether leaving kids of that age alone in the dark would be the right thing to do. Then he noticed their eyes.

Their eyeballs were totally black, with no visible iris, as if they were full of jet-black ink. "You need to let us in; we can't come in unless you ask us. You can't leave us out here," they repeated. He ignored them and sped off, and as he looked back in his mirrors, he saw that they had disappeared. Shaken by the incident, he posted a description on a local message board and it wasn't long before his story was picked up nationwide. Several other sightings were reported up and down the country, all of them involving young children knocking on doors and windows of cars and houses, asking to be let in for food and becoming quietly insistent when they were denied access. Nobody knows what would happen if you beckoned them inside, because the only people who did were sadly unable to tell the tale.

HOME ALONE

British newspapers reported the mysterious case of a girl who was spending the day at home alone after her school was closed due to a snowstorm. She was watching TV in the living room when she noticed something out of the corner of her eye, in the glass doors that led out into the garden. There was a man standing in the bushes, staring directly at her. She screamed, and immediately sprang off the sofa and ran out of the room to call the police. When she got through, she told them that there was an intruder in her garden, and the operator told her to make sure all the doors and windows were locked. Officers were on their way but would be delayed by the snow on the roads.

She was terrified—she couldn't remember whether the patio doors were locked or not—and it took all the courage she could muster to tiptoe back into the living room and check if the man was still in the garden. She couldn't see him, and she quickly locked the doors. She endured an agonising wait by the front door until two policemen arrived. They told her that they were already searching for a dangerous suspect responsible for an assault in another home in the area and went outside to check the garden. To their confusion, they found that there were no footprints, despite the thick snow covering the grass. When they returned to the living room, they saw what they were looking for: a set of wet footprints behind the sofa. "You were very lucky, young lady. He was standing right behind you—what you saw was his reflection in the glass."

THE CRYING BABY

A woman was working late at her office in the city when she was interrupted by a strange noise coming from outside her window. As it got louder, she recognized the unmistakable sound of a baby crying—an unusual noise at that time of night in that part of town, where there were few houses. She looked out of the window and couldn't see anything, but the crying continued, and it sounded almost as if it were inside the building. She checked downstairs, where the noise was so loud that it could only have been coming from right outside the front door.

She put her hand on the door handle but despite all her instincts telling her to help the baby, something stopped her from opening it. Instead, she called the police and described the situation, asking them if they knew anything about a missing baby. She didn't get the answer she expected, as the police officer told her not to open the door under any circumstances, to move away from the windows and to wait for help to arrive. The woman took this to mean that a missing child had indeed been reported and put the phone down. She moved away from the windows and waited. But the crying continued to get louder and she began to wonder why she should wait for the police— after all, they could take hours to arrive and the baby might need urgent medical attention; it must have been getting cold out there. She decided that she would bring the poor child inside and then wait for the police, so she opened the door and stepped out onto the street. The crying stopped, but she could see no signs of a baby. The next sounds she heard were her own screams. When the police finally arrived, they found her lifeless body on the street, her throat slashed. If she had stayed on the phone long enough, the police officer would have had time to explain that there was a serial killer on the loose in town who was luring women outside at night with the recorded sound of a crying baby.

DON'T PLAY THE LOTTERY

The police department of a small town in Australia put out an online message warning residents about an unknown man who was suspected of killing one homeowner, seriously wounding another and trespassing on several other people's property. He was dubbed the Lottery Killer because of his particular method of approaching his targets and murdering them. The first thing the victim would notice was a figure, with his face obscured, standing somewhere where he could clearly be seen, late at night. He would pick houses with glass doors or large windows overlooking the street, which he would stand in front of, silhouetted against the street lights and waiting to be noticed by the occupants— sometimes for several hours. Then he would knock 13 times at the door and wait for a response. If spoken to, he wouldn't respond, but if the door was opened, he would attack viciously and indiscriminately with a long knife, murdering people in their own home. A bloody lottery ticket was left on the bodies.

THE GORBALS VAMPIRE

The children waited until it was dark to sneak out of their homes, picking up sticks and rocks to use as weapons on their way to the cemetery. They stalked the gravestones all night, waiting for a sight of what they had come to flush out: the Gorbals Vampire.

The Gorbals area of Glasgow, Scotland, had been terrorised by stories of a 7-foot-tall vampire with metal teeth who preyed on children and had already eaten two local boys. The rumors were so powerful that gangs of hysterical kids took to the cemetery in the south of the city to catch the monster, despite efforts by the police to stop them. Frightened parents pestered the authorities, wanting to know if there really was a child-eating bloodsucking murderer roaming the place. To alleviate their fears, the authorities blamed the new comics from America, which were full of horror stories, for whipping up wild ideas in young minds and even went as far as banning sensationalist publications. However, the local children suspected that the adults were lying and were also terrified of the iron-fanged fiend. They were sure that he wasn't some imagined monster from a comic book: the vampire was real and they were going to find him.

The sprawling Victorian cemetery looked like the perfect lair for an undead creature of the night: home to more than a quarter of a million dead bodies, its crumbling statues and sunken gravestones were lit at night by the flames of a nearby steelworks. The children scrambled over a seven-foot wall and dropped down amongst the graves, speaking in whispers. Then someone shouted, "There he is!" as a shadow flashed quickly across a tomb. The children gave frantic chase, tumbling over headstones in the dark and brandishing makeshift weapons. Soon they came upon a great stone mausoleum, its door ajar. Peering into the murky depths of the tomb, they could make out a large stone coffin in the corner, with its heavy marble lid pushed to one side. Was this the beast's hiding place? A couple of the braver kids, egged on by the others, edged inside the building and fearfully poked their sticks inside the dark sarcophagus. The rest of the gang held their breath, unsure whether they would stay and fight or run for their lives if the creature was awoken. But no attack came; the tomb was empty. Clearly, the vampire had escaped their grasp once again, but his hunters vowed to return the next night—and the next, if necessary—armed with wooden stakes.

THE BUNNY MAN

There is a tunnel under a road that runs through remote woods in Oregon; an insane asylum had been built in the vicinity not long after the Civil War. As the area was colonised and became more popular, houses were built around the asylum, and near the turn of the century, the residents started to question its existence.

When an escaped patient attacked a child, the authorities finally decided to close the institution.

They loaded the patients onto buses to transfer them to alternative places, but one of the vehicles crashed in the woods after a violent passenger broke free of his chains and attacked the driver. All were later apprehended, except for two: Billy Smith and Michael Wood. Police and dogs combed the forest, and picked up a trail marked with the mutilated bodies of rabbits, some half-eaten. The trail led down the old wagon track to the bridge, where they found one of the missing patients; Michael Wood was hanging inside the tunnel. He had been bludgeoned to death and his ears had been removed. Attached to his foot was a note that read: "You'll never catch the bunny man!"

They attributed the murder to Billy Smith, supposedly a friend of Wood and convicted of several violent crimes against animals. The search continued but Billy, or Bunny Man as the cops had taken to calling him, was never found. The only traces he possibly left behind were the rabbits nailed to trees that hunters would occasionally find on overgrown paths, which they put down to a macabre joke. Although Billy Smith was eventually forgotten, the story of the Bunny Man was passed down through generations of locals, and the tunnel became the place to be for bored teenagers, who would dare themselves to stay there until midnight.

In 1965 a group of teens had congregated at the bridge on Halloween. Seven remained until midnight, but one of the girls decided to walk home just before then and wandered away, back down the track to the main road. A moment later she looked back and saw a bright flash of light coming from under the bridge, even though there were no cars or people on the road, and then she heard her friends screaming at the top of their lungs. Soon there was nothing but silence and darkness. Terrified, she ran home.

The next day, all of the teens who had remained under the bridge at midnight were discovered hanged with their ears cut off. The police found a dismembered rabbit nailed to a tree nearby, along with a note that said, "Don't forget the Bunny Man!"

They never managed to identify a suspect, never mind the murderer.

Years later a teenager and his girlfriend had driven down there in search of some privacy—if you pulled off the main road and down an old track, nobody could see your car under the bridge. They both knew the legends—they had heard them since kindergarten—but nobody was scared of them anymore. It was a bright summer night, with a full moon, and the place was indeed full of rabbits, which stopped in the car's headlights and stared as the pair drove under the bridge.

The pair soon lost track of time and at midnight they didn't notice the rabbits streaming under the bridge, as if running from a predator; they only looked up when they saw a flash of light. The next person who saw them was a man searching for his dog that had run off to chase the local rabbits. The teens were swinging from the roof of the bridge, their ears missing. As the pet owner stared in shock at the grisly sight, the dog brought him a piece of paper in his mouth. It said, "You'll never catch the Bunny Man!"

THE MASSACRE

In 2007 an Ohio newspaper reported the rumors buzzing around a local university campus. A famous psychic had appeared on a phone-in radio show, claiming to have heard predictions at a séance. She warned that a massacre would take place at the college on Halloween and that, by the end of the month, seven students would die in a large H-shaped building near a railroad track on an Ohio campus. Students made frantic phone calls to university administrators, who in turn called in the police to investigate the claims but were reassured that there was no substance to the rumors. Nonetheless, extra officers were deployed to help the regular campus cops. The student paper reported that some students were genuinely in fear of an attack, and many had taken refuge off campus until the threat was over. Soon it was the last weekend of the month and the college drinking society was due to hold a party. To show that they weren't scared by the rumors, they decided that it would have a serial killer theme. Students who had not taken flight turned up wearing costumes from horror movies, and the venue was deliberately chosen because it was located in an H-shaped building. Halfway through the party there was a blackout and the drunken students joked that it would be the perfect time for the psychic's attacker to strike. When the lights came back on, though, nobody was laughing: seven students lay dead, killed with an axe to the head in the bathroom.

WHERE'S MY LIVER?

Bobby had been told by his mother to go to the shops and pick up a packet of fresh liver from the butcher's. His grandfather was coming for dinner, and liver and onions was his favorite dish. Bobby hated liver, and he hated going in the butcher's, but he did as he was told and set off to the shops. On the way there he met a friend who invited him to play a new computer game at his house, with some other mates.

Bobby wanted to explain that he was running an errand for his mother but he was too embarrassed, so he accepted; after all, it wouldn't take long. When he next checked the time, he realized that it was dark and all the shops would probably be shut. He shot out of the house and ran down the road to the butcher's, which was indeed closed. He was wondering what he would say to his mother, when he saw an old man rummaging around in the bins to the rear of the shop. He looked like a tramp, with greasy grey hair plastered over his dirty skin. Next to him was a supermarket trolley filled with filthy bags. The man saw him, and though Bobby wanted to run away, he was curious, so he asked the man what he was looking for.

"I've been getting myself some meat," he told the boy, evidently pleased with himself. "They throw out perfectly good stuff here every day," he added, pointing at the bins. Bobby saw that he had filled his trolley with lumps of meat wrapped in paper and on top was a fat calf's liver. Before the old man could react, he grabbed it and ran off home as fast as he could. All the way down the high street Bobby could hear the trolley squeaking after him, but there was no way such an old man could keep up with a young boy.

The liver went down a treat, and Bobby's grandfather said it was the best he'd eaten for as long as he could remember. The boy was allowed to stay up late that night as a reward and he played computer games downstairs until the small hours, pleased with his actions. As he was walking up the stairs to bed, he heard a noise outside the front door, so he looked out of the window but there was nothing there. Then came a squeaking sound, unmistakably the noise of an old supermarket trolley. Still he could see nothing, but the noise grew louder and when the trolley came into view, Bobby ran upstairs in terror and hid under the blankets. He didn't dare look out of the window to see if the old man was there and, eventually, he fell asleep. He was woken later by a knock on his bedroom door, followed by silence. A voice hissed, "Where's my liver?" Then again, louder, "Where's my liver, boy?" Bobby was frozen to the spot, and although he tried to scream, no noise came out. The door handle turned and the old man from the butcher's stood in the doorway, smiling in the darkness. He was flashing a meat cleaver. "There's my liver!"

THE BRIDGE

There is a bridge in Wales where thrill-seeking teenagers go on Halloween. It's a pretty little humpback stone bridge spanning a rocky river that flows down from the mountains, but it has a sinister past.

Many years ago, there was a young woman—an only child—who lived in a manor house up the valley. She was smart and headstrong, and refused to marry the men that her father found for her, so he kept her locked away, waiting for her to agree to do his bidding. One day a relative visited in a brand new motor car: a rare machine at the time in that part of the country. Her father had let his daughter out of her room for the occasion, so she took her one opportunity to escape. When her father wasn't looking, the girl leapt into the driver's seat and sped off down the valley. She flew down the hill towards the river, enjoying a blissful minute of freedom, before she realized that she didn't know how to stop the vehicle and she ploughed straight off the bridge onto the rocks below.

Now, many years later, it's still said that she haunts that bridge. If you flash your headlights as you're driving over it, your car will stall. If you're lucky, it will start again in few moments and you can be on your way but if you're not, you will hear the girl knocking on the window. If you don't open a door to let the girl in, you will die in a car accident within a week. The girl never managed to escape over the bridge and she won't let you escape either...

POP CULTURE

HAIR METAL

In 1972 the rock band Led Zeppelin landed at an airport in Singapore for a long-awaited show on the island. As they were preparing to disembark, the band's management informed them that they were not allowed to set foot on the runway because of the government's attitude to 1970s-style long hair. The authorities in charge associated their flowing locks with bad behavior and moral decay, and did not want the decadent Western rockers to lead their impressionable young astray. Shocked, the band agreed to stay on the plane and took off for another, more welcoming, destination.

THE FIFTH BEATLE?

One of the most popular and bizarre conspiracy theories in the world of music is the idea that Paul McCartney actually died many years ago and was replaced with an imposter: the lucky winner of a Paul McCartney lookalike contest. A rumor began in 1967, not unlike today's Twitter hoaxes, which claimed that the singer had died in a car accident the previous year. While most people received this announcement with a dose of scepticism, it was enough to convince superstitious fans of the band to pore over artwork and lyrics, looking for secret meanings and spreading the idea that he really was dead. By 1969, the unbelievable story was being discussed across America in magazines and on the radio.

Believers of the strange tale cited many different so-called facts, such as the mysterious messages left by the band about McCartney on their records, which can only be heard by playing them backwards, including John Lennon apparently saying, "I buried Paul" towards the end of "Strawberry Fields Forever." Also, McCartney appears on the cover of the group's 1969 *Abbey Road* album with no shoes on and out of step with the other members, leading fans to wonder why he had been singled out as different. Ringo Starr is dressed in black—clothing similar to what is worn by an undertaker—and George is all in denim, reminiscent of a gravedigger. The fact that John Lennon is dressed all in white, like an angel, reinforced the theme of life and death. McCartney, seemingly very much alive, gave an interview to *Life* magazine later in the year, but it wasn't enough to convince fans that he was the real deal. Many pointed to yet more clues as to the singer's demise: the original cover art for the album *Yesterday and Today* featured bloody, dismembered body parts, supposedly a reference to McCartney's death, and close comparisons of dated photographs apparently revealed subtle signs that he had been replaced with a similar-looking imposter, who had undergone extensive plastic surgery to look like the star. Despite all the evidence to the contrary, many fans have never given up on the idea that today's Paul McCartney is not who he says he is.

THE KING

Early in January 2015 an internet news site posted a story about a homeless man who had been found dead underneath a bridge in San Diego, California. The man's true identity was a mystery, and the authorities didn't give it much thought, as many unidentified vagrants are found dead each year in the city. Local homeless people interviewed by the single policeman on the case reported that he was a familiar face in the underground community, known variously as Tommy, Jessie or Vern, depending on whom you asked. He used to boast that he had been on the streets for decades.

The coroner processed the man's DNA through the system as a matter of routine, not expecting anything interesting to come to light. The name "Presley" came up and this amused the technician, who joked that they'd finally found The King. Then somebody noticed that the body actually resembled vaguely what Elvis Presley might have looked like had he not died in the 1970s. The coroner's office couldn't believe what they had found, but the tests don't lie, so they shared their findings with the police and the FBI.

Fans of Presley have long had doubts about his demise, with some believing that he faked his own death and escaped to South America. Presley spelled his middle name Aron, but for some reason it became "Aaron" on his headstone—was that the mistake that exposed the conspiracy? Hundreds of people claimed to have spotted The King in various places around the world, from Mississippi to Sweden, but had he finally been found—dead for real this time—in California? It was also speculated that the man found under the San Diego bridge was not actually The King, but his twin brother, Jessie, who was thought to have died at birth. The technicians never heard anything more about the body, and the coroner told them to keep it to themselves.

I'M A (PIRATE) SLAVE 4 U

British merchant ships off the coast of Somalia have been deploying an unusual weapon in their fight against pirates raiding vessels in small boats: pop music—more specifically, Britney Spears's pop music. On the advice of their security teams, ships passing the east coast of Africa have been using loudspeakers to blast out Britney's jaunty pop hits to deter pirates, including "Oops! I Did It Again" and "Toxic." A security official told a newspaper that Britney's recordings were their first choice, as they had been told that the pirates would hate them the most. The approach is similar to that undertaken by security services interrogating terrorist suspects in places like Iraq and Afghanistan; there they have played Christina Aguilera songs to break down suspects.

THE REVOLUTIONARY BALLET DANCER

You've probably heard of the world-famous ballet dancer Dame Margot Fonteyn, but you may not know that she was suspected of plotting to overthrow the government of Panama in 1959. Recently revealed secrets from the British government archive revealed that she was one of the key conspirators in a plot to land men and guns to help take over the country. Her husband was a member of the political opposition and a gun smuggler, who used a fishing trip with Dame Margot as cover to land his illicit cargo ashore as part of a plan led by the Cuban revolutionary Fidel Castro. The Panamanian Army rumbled the operation, so the ballet dancer used her yacht to lead the government off the scent. It didn't work, and she was arrested and jailed overnight.

On her return to London, she acted as if what happened had been a minor misunderstanding and smiled for the press. The British ambassador explained that he did not regard her conduct "as fitting in any British subject," but nevertheless she was soon back on the guest list of all the best high society parties and eventually returned to Panama, where she died in 1991.

LOVE ROLLERCOASTER

In 1975 the Ohio Players released "Love Rollercoaster," a funk track that would later be covered by the Red Hot Chili Peppers. If you listen closely to the end of the first verse, you'll hear a strange high-pitched noise in the background that doesn't fit with the rest of the music. It sounds eerily like the blood-curdling scream of a terrified woman. Fans speculated for years over what was behind the noise, and many think it's the sound of a genuine murder. Some say a terrible crime occurred in the studio when the band were recording the song, whereas others claim that it was inserted by a sound engineer at a later stage as a sick joke. Another version of events is inspired by the album cover, which features erotic images of a woman covered in what appears to be honey but was actually hot wax or plastic; many suspected that the cry was in fact the model screaming in pain as the substance was removed. The band would not comment on the noise when journalists brought up the subject.

TOP GUY

Tom Cruise has saved countless heroines from certain death on the big screen, but it's less well known that he has also helped to save the lives of several mere mortals in real life. At one of his packed-out movie premieres, the assembled fans were so wild that people were starting to be crushed against the barriers. Cruise reached into the crowd and pulled to safety two young boys who were struggling to breathe.

Moreover, he once witnessed a hit-and-run accident and although he didn't literally save the victim, he called an ambulance and stayed with her until she got to hospital. When he learned that she didn't have medical insurance, he gave her several thousands of dollars to pay for her care.

Even when he is on vacation, he isn't off duty. Relaxing on a super yacht in the Mediterranean, Cruise spotted a boat on fire nearby so wasted no time in sending a launch over to rescue all five crewmembers from the burning wreckage, just before it sank.

LIGHTS, CAMERA, ACTION

A Hollywood action movie filmed in Hungary saw some unscripted action when the country's anti-terrorist SWAT squad—in full battle gear—raided the film's set after a tip-off and confiscated the guns that the actors were supposed to be using. The film company thought they had bought fakes, but they were duped. They had in fact brought 85 fully functional semi-automatic weapons onto the set, which would have been lethal if used with live ammunition.

THREE MEN AND A GHOST

The next time the movie *Three Men and a Baby* is repeated on television, take a closer look at the long continuous shot where Jack and his mother walk through the men's apartment. You won't spot it on first viewing, but if you slow the shot down and look again, you can make out what appears to be a rifle and then a boy with a blank look on his face, peering at the actors from behind some curtains. It doesn't look like it's supposed to be in the film, and it has freaked out viewers for years. Rumor has it that, unbeknown to the film's production crew, the apartment where the shot was filmed had been the scene of a violent murder several years previously. A man used a hunting rifle to kill a young boy, whose spirit haunted the apartment during filming, and was said to have appeared at cinemas where the movie was shown.

OMENS OF THE OMEN

The 1976 movie *The Omen,* which describes the birth of the Antichrist within a privileged American family, is widely regarded as one of the creepiest films ever made; and it's not just what you see on the screen that scares people.

The bad omens started when the movie's star, Gregory Peck, and screenwriter, David Seltzer, each took separate flights to Britain for filming: both planes were hit by lightning, foreshadowing the death of a priest in the film, who is killed by a falling lightning rod. Then the film's production team booked a plane to use during the shoot, but swapped for another at the last minute. The aircraft that they had intended to take crashed shortly after take-off on its next flight, leaving no survivors.

Members of *The Omen* film crew also narrowly escaped harm when the IRA bombed a London restaurant during filming, and an animal handler for the film was later reportedly attacked and eaten by his own lions. Similarly, one of the stuntmen on the film suffered a near fatal accident when working on his next job.

A wedding scene in the movie was filmed inside Guildford Cathedral, making the locals too frightened to enter the site for years after the movie was released and causing a steep drop in visitors. Many years later a mentally ill man was shot by police outside the church.

Perhaps the creepiest coincidence related to *The Omen*, though, concerns the movie's special effects designer, responsible for the famous death scene when a pane of glass decapitates a character as it falls off a truck. A few months after the premiere of the movie he was involved in a major car accident while on holiday, where he witnessed his travel companion being decapitated in an eerily similar fashion.

You would think all that would be enough to make Hollywood think twice about remaking the film, but remake it they did in 2006. It didn't take long for problems to start: filming took place in Eastern Europe, where the locals didn't take kindly to the content and vandalized the sets. A member of the crew was involved in a car accident, where, unbelievably, part of the number plate read "666." The film's cameras were plagued by technical malfunctions, which the crew referred to as the "666 error," and they eventually lost a whole day's filming. Unsurprisingly, there are no more remakes of *The Omen* in the pipeline.

SHE'S IN THE TV

In the horror film *Poltergeist* (1982), a malevolent spirit haunts a family who have moved into a house built on a Native American burial ground. The film is loosely based on a frightening incident reported in 1950s New York, where a ghost terrified a family in their home, causing objects to fly around rooms, mirrors to be broken and bottles to burst in the kitchen. The supernatural events were witnessed by a police officer who attended the scene and was almost decapitated by a globe that was hurled at him by an invisible force. Paranormal investigators could find no answer to the mystery. The family consulted ministers from a variety of religions, who conducted various rituals to exorcise the spirit without any success. Then suddenly, as quickly as it had started, the haunting stopped.

In the film the ghost sucks the young daughter in the family into purgatory via the television screen but if the stories told about what happened behind the scenes of the movie and its many sequels are only half true, then it wasn't just the TV that was cursed.

Child star Heather O'Rourke played the girl trapped in the television in all three films, but only lived to see two of them. She was plagued with health problems and survived a heart attack after a bout of flu but in February 1988, 12-year-old O'Rourke died during surgery to fix a stomach problem.

Actor Lou Perryman, who played Pugsley in the original movie, was killed in 2009 in a brutal axe murder at his home in Texas. Julian Beck, who played a sinister preacher in *Poltergeist II*, died before the film was released. Will Sampson, who portrayed a Native American shaman in the same movie, did not survive a heart transplant.

The writer of a book accompanying the film claimed that his office was struck by lightning and the arcade games in his collection began to play of their own accord. *Poltergeist* was remade in 2015, and it is not known whether the people involved were aware of the chequered past of the franchise.

HOW TO RUIN YOUR CHILDHOOD

Is it true that some of these beloved kid's films are not quite as wholesome as we thought?

A Claim Denied by Disney

Disney movies are rightly treasured the world over by parents looking for something fun, wholesome and family-friendly to keep their children entertained. Occasionally, however, questionable images slip through the net, and Mum and Dad might be a little shocked by what little Johnny is watching.

The castle on the cover of the videotape of *The Little Mermaid* was thought by some to resemble a man's sexual organ, and some parents were so worried about its effect on their children that they filed legal complaints against stores selling the tape. It's not entirely clear whether it was intentional or not, but Disney eventually changed the cover.

In *Aladdin* there is a scene featuring Jasmine and her tiger where the star allegedly tells teenagers to strip off, apparently saying, "Good teenagers take off your clothes." Although the official line is: "C'mon...good kitty. Take off and go," it doesn't sound like that in the movie, and the source of the confusion is a mystery.

Legend says that in *Who Framed Roger Rabbit*, animators included frames where Jessica Rabbit's nether regions can be seen when she is thrown from a car. It didn't come to wider attention until the videotape was released and people could look closely at the film.

In the 1990s Disney recalled millions of copies of the 1970s film *The Rescuers*, in which two mice go on an adventure to save a girl trapped by a villain, after it was discovered that one frame of the animated movie featured a real photograph of a naked woman. It was inserted as a joke during post-production for the original release in cinemas, as it could not be seen when the film was viewed at normal speed, but they forgot to remove it when the movie was put out on tape, and the single offending frame could be viewed using the pause button.

Disney made a nature documentary about creatures of the Arctic Circle in the 1950s called *White Wilderness*, in which the belief that lemmings are stupid and kill themselves en masse by jumping off cliffs is explored. As these creatures do not really kill themselves when they migrate—that one really *is* an urban myth—the film crew had to improvise. They flew a colony of lemmings across Canada and put them on a cliff edge, expecting them to jump off. When they wouldn't co-operate, the film-makers pushed them to their deaths so they could get the footage they required, with the voice-over explaining that they mistook the sea for a lake they could swim across. It didn't stop them winning an Oscar for the film, though.

We're Not in Kansas Any More

Next time you watch the old *Wizard of Oz* movie from 1939, watch out for someone creepy in the background when Dorothy dances down the yellow brick road with the Scarecrow and Tin Man. It's said that one of the dwarfs hired to play a Munchkin in the movie went mad during filming after one of the actresses rejected his advances and hanged himself on set. If you look closely, you can apparently see him dangling from a tree at the back of the picture. There is also another well-known oddity about the film: if you play Pink Floyd's album *The Dark Side of the Moon* along with the movie, the music synchronises with the film in creepy ways. When the Scarecrow—who requires a brain—dances down the yellow brick road, the song "Brain Damage" plays, with the lyrics "keep the loonies on the path." The lyrics "You lock the door and throw away the key" in the song "Breathe" can be heard as the film shows the door of the castle in which Dorothy is locked up. Moreover, during the same Pink Floyd song, when the Tin Man sings "If I Only Had a Heart," the rhythm of the rock music sounds like a heartbeat.

The Lion King

In 1995 a religious group in America put out a newsletter warning of inappropriate sexual content in *The Lion King*. Apparently, at the point when the film's hero, Simba, lies on the edge of a rocky outcrop at night, the dust that swirls around him in the sky spells out the word "sex." Others maintain it says "SFX," standing for special effects, but it's a close call. One of the film's other characters got into trouble when a talking book of the movie was released, in which animals spoke when buttons were pressed. Parents thought that Rafiki the baboon said, "Squashed bananas up your arse" when prompted.

King of the Jungle

In 1918 the very first Tarzan movie came to the big screen. *Tarzan of the Apes* starred Elmo Lincoln as the king of the jungle, and the actor claimed that he took the role perhaps a little too seriously. In the climactic scene, a lion attacks Tarzan and Jane in a hut, only for Tarzan to stab the beast heroically to death. The scene, featuring a real lion, is over in a flash, as much of the footage was lost. Lincoln claimed that he had really killed the lion, and that its body was stuffed and displayed in the theatre lobby when the movie premiered on Broadway.

MEDICAL

DEAD BANGING

In 2013 overzealous heavy metal fans were warned by authorities of the dangers of vigorous headbanging—the custom of shaking one's head to the rhythms of Motörhead or Metallica—because the practice had been linked to serious brain injuries. It was reported that a German fan required treatment after banging his head too vigorously at a Motörhead show. The middle-aged heavy-metal enthusiast enjoyed a night of skull shaking but suffered from increasingly painful headaches for a month afterwards, leading to a scan which revealed bleeding in the brain that required immediate surgery. The rock fan was lucky to survive, but medical experts were surprised to discover that brain hemorrhages caused by headbanging had happened on more than one occasion in medical history, and some were fatal. It was rumored that an AC/DC fan from London succumbed to the condition during a performance of the song "Brain Shake" at Wembley Arena.

FIREWORKS

A blind young man named Paolo from South America was visiting his cousins in Rio de Janeiro for New Year's Eve and enjoying a street party as the coming year was welcomed across the city. Once the clock struck midnight, fireworks shot across the sky; as he smelled the familiar sulphur and heard the sounds of the explosions, he felt a stabbing pain in the side of his head and saw a flash of colors before he blacked out. When the boy came to in hospital, he got two large surprises: he could see and he had sneezed out a small shiny metal object covered in blood. It was a bullet. To say it was a mystery would be an understatement, but the police eventually cracked the puzzle. As was the New Year's custom in the area, the local ranchers and cowboys fired their rifles into the sky at midnight, after imbibing a tad too much local liquor, and one stray round had returned to earth and entered Paolo's head through the top of his skull. The bullet passed behind his eyes, hit his nasal bone and lodged itself in his nostril, grazing a nerve that meant he could now see—and all without causing any lasting damage.

GAS ATTACK

Authorities blamed an unusual diet and a lack of ventilation for the death of a morbidly obese man found dead at his home in Florida. Neighbors hadn't seen or heard the man for several days and alerted the police, knowing that he was unwell. Doctors first assumed that he had died as a result of his bulk, but the first paramedics on the scene noted that the room was full of a foul odor that left them unable to breathe. They had to be hospitalized after collapsing due to the smell. The man had produced so much methane gas from his own flatulence in his small, unventilated room that he had suffocated in his sleep. A post-mortem revealed dangerous levels of gas still in his system, and large amounts of beans and Brussels sprouts—his favorite foods—in his stomach.

FOOD GOES TO YOUR HEAD

People always say that you should immerse yourself in the local culture when you visit a new country, and at the very least you should try the food. Sometimes, however, it's right to be wary about what you're eating on your trips to exotic destinations. An American woman who had recently returned from South America was ill for weeks. She rightly assumed that she had picked up something nasty when she was abroad, but she didn't know what. Then she began to suffer violent seizures. When doctors scanned her brain, they found a lesion of some sort, which had to be investigated to establish whether it was cancerous. She underwent a six-hour procedure that had to be performed while she was awake, as it was such a sensitive area of the brain. Her doctors were shocked to discover that a parasitic tapeworm had burrowed inside her brain tissue, causing damaging inflammation. If such swellings become too big or are in the wrong place, they can cause the blood flow to the brain to be cut off. They were able to remove the worm from the woman's head and she made a full recovery. Doctors believe that the parasite entered her body after she ate a pork taco on vacation. The tapeworm spreads as a result of poor hygiene when preparing food, thus allowing its eggs to enter the human gut and develop into a worm, which then travels through the bloodstream and, if you're particularly unlucky, burrows itself into the brain.

A DONATION

A German man was visiting Thailand for a business conference and staying in a plush hotel in Bangkok with his colleagues. On the last night of his trip, he was winding down with other attendees, sharing a few drinks in the hotel bar. He had asked the barman if he had any tips for places to go for a good night out in the city, but was told that it wasn't safe at that time of year for foreigners. He wasn't convinced, but a particularly nervous workmate persuaded him to stay in the hotel bar, especially as the bartender was offering drinks on the house.

The cocktails started flowing and soon he was feeling a little tipsier than normal, but he put that down to being stressed out and tired after the business meetings. His nervous workmate bid him goodnight and turned in, reminding him that he had a flight to catch in the morning. However, by then an attractive local girl had started asking the man questions and buying him more drinks, so he barely noticed the advice.

The last thing he remembered of that night was telling a joke about his suffering liver after his colleagues had disappeared upstairs.

The first thing he felt the next morning was excruciating pain, not in his head, but in his back. He was shivering in a bath full of ice, colored red from blood—his own blood, he discovered to his horror, as he noticed a tube protruding from his back. Around his neck was a note written in German, "Call the embassy or you die," with the embassy number. There was a phone within reach and he dialled with shaking hands. He told the woman on the other end of the line where he was and described his situation; she asked calmly whether there was a tube in his back, as if this was a regular occurrence. When he confirmed there was, she told him not to move under any circumstances and explained that paramedics were on their way. Both of his kidneys had been removed.

FUNERAL FIRE

The work of an undertaker is generally pretty straightforward, and their clients are usually not ones to cause trouble, but sometimes the human body can throw up surprises. When it comes to cremations, the larger the person, the longer and hotter the fire will burn. When a 60-stone man was cremated in Virginia, USA, his bulk was too much for even the specialist equipment to handle. As the temperature rose, his body fat melted and human grease leaked out of the oven, causing the building to become engulfed in flames. Firefighters had to be called to oversee the cremation to the end.

Similarly, a particularly large Austrian woman also caused a building fire when she was being cremated, sparking calls for a weight limit for health and safety reasons. Switzerland, on the other hand, always precise, ensures that overweight deceased persons are handled by a specialist facility built to withstand the extra heat.

SCIENCE IS DANGEROUS

One day in July 1978, a Russian scientist studying for a PhD at the Institute for High Energy Physics near Moscow was performing maintenance on a particle accelerator. The machine was the largest in the Soviet Union, using electromagnetic fields to fire particles through a giant tube at speeds close to the speed of light. Something went wrong with the safety procedure and a beam of charged particles shot right through the scientist's head, giving him a dose of radiation thousands of times higher than a human should be able to survive. Despite seeing a flash "brighter than a thousand suns," he felt no pain.

The left-hand side of his head, where protons travelling at nearly the speed of light had entered, had swelled until he could not be recognized. The burned skin eventually peeled away, revealing the path of burned tissue and bone that the particles had seared through his head, as they entered through a nostril and exited through the back of his skull. Although he had survived the event, doctors expected that he would soon succumb to the high levels of radiation and suffer a lingering death.

However, he didn't die. He made an almost complete recovery, with only hearing problems and some facial paralysis to show for his ordeal. His brain worked normally, although he did tire a little quicker, and he was able to complete his PhD studies and start a family. The narrow beam of protons had passed through his brain without harming the vital tissue—a similar technology is used today in radiotherapy to destroy cancer cells without harming healthy tissue.

IT'S A BOY!

Scientists have discovered that a 3,000-year-old pregnancy test used by the ancient Egyptians was remarkably accurate. Expectant mothers would pee on pieces of barley and wheat: if the barley grain sprouted, they were pregnant with a boy, whereas if the wheat sprouted, then it was a girl. Recent tests have found that it was probably 70 per cent accurate.

Techniques hadn't progressed much by the 1920s, but scientists discovered that they could tell whether a woman was pregnant by the presence of a chemical produced by the placenta. The only way to test for this substance was to inject the patient's urine into the veins of animals, usually mice. Then the ovaries of the rodents would be removed and tested for the chemical. Of course, the mice died.

Thankfully, it was discovered that there was another option. The prospective mother would give a urine sample, which was then injected into an unsuspecting African clawed frog. If the animal produced eggs within one day then the woman was pregnant. The benefit of this test was that they didn't have to kill the frog to get the result, as one creature could be tested repeatedly. The test was widely used until the 1960s, when new techniques that didn't involve amphibians were developed.

THE MAN WITH TWO FACES

A disturbing video once made the rounds on the internet. In the clip, doctors are treating a hideously deformed man who has what appears to be a second face on the back of his head, complete with a mouth, which opened in tandem with the other, tongue, teeth and other crude facial features. It was said that the man was Chang Tzu Ping, who lived as a hermit in a remote Chinese village, too terrified to show his face to the world. The local children would jeer and throw rocks when he left the house. In the 1970s, he was discovered by a troop of American soldiers who rescued him from his tormentors and took him back to the States, where his second face was removed in a 12-hour operation as part of a diplomatic deal. It's speculated that his case may have been an example of "fetus in fetu": an extremely rare condition occurring in multiple pregnancies when one embryo becomes stuck inside the other and grows inside its twin.

SELF-SURGERY

In 1961 the only doctor at a remote Russian Antarctic research station fell ill with what he suspected was appendicitis. He hoped it would get better on its own, as the nearest Russian base was 1,000 miles away and a blizzard had been raging for days, preventing any possible rescue by aircraft. When the pain became excruciating and he developed a fever, he knew he had only one option: remove his own appendix before it burst and killed him. The 27-year-old enlisted a driver and a scientist as ad hoc theatre nurses, and propped himself up in bed. He numbed the affected area with a local anesthetic, and he set to work slicing into his own stomach and removing the inflamed organ, while his assistants held up a mirror so he could see his handiwork. Despite his scalpel slipping and cutting into part of his gut, he completed the operation in two hours and was back on duty within a couple of weeks, becoming a hero of the Soviet Union.

DO-IT-YOURSELF

One American surgeon working in the early twentieth century was not what you would consider your typical physician: he tattooed newborn babies—not for decoration, but so that they would not get mixed up with other babies in the hospital. The mother would be marked with an identical tattoo so that she could forever identify her child. He also took to putting his signature on patients on which he had successfully operated, leaving his initials tattooed on their body. He was most renowned for performing surgeries on himself, though. In 1919, after one of his fingers became infected, rather than call on the services of one of his colleagues, he set to work amputating the digit himself. However, this was child's play compared to his future experiments. A couple of years later when he came down with appendicitis—and you can see where this is going—he decided to test whether he could remove his appendix himself, blazing the path that a Soviet doctor later followed, using only a local anesthetic. The surgeon who had been planning to do the job was understandably shocked, but as the patient was the chief surgeon at the hospital, and his boss, there wasn't much he could do about it. The eccentric physician wasted no time in injecting drugs into his abdomen and slicing open his own stomach, removing the appendix with the help of mirrors in less than half an hour. He was back operating on other people within two weeks. The next time he required a surgical procedure, this time for a hernia at the age of 72, he picked up the scalpel once again. Although this tricky procedure required him to cut extremely close to the femoral artery, he laughed and joked with the nurses as he completed it in two hours. As he tired towards the end of the operation, he finally allowed his colleague to stitch him back up.

HISTORICAL

ISLAND WARFARE

On 15 August 1943 American forces fighting the Japanese prepared to invade Kiska, a small island in the North Pacific between Alaska and Russia. Japanese forces had invaded the island, as well as another nearby, one year earlier in order to protect Japanese territory in the area. The United States responded with an aerial bombardment and naval blockade, determined to drive the Japanese from the territory, but they stayed put, leaving as the only option an invasion of ground forces to take on an estimated 5,000 Japanese marines. American and Canadian troops landed en masse on 15 August, determined to retake the island but, to their amazement, nobody was there.

Several weeks previously, US forces had retaken the neighboring island and the Japanese, intimidated, had decided to make a secret retreat from Kiska. They left under the cover of night and heavy fog, without anybody noticing. As a result, the Allied forces were tasked with invading an empty island; in the process they lost more than 100 men and suffered hundreds of casualties after they fired on each other, booby traps left by the Japanese were triggered and a destroyer struck an underwater mine.

FASCIST FOREST?

In a small rural German town not far from Berlin, which had started to forget the horrors that occurred decades previously, the country's dark past emerged in the early 1990s when a plane flew over to take aerial images. The aircraft went past a heavily wooded area, dominated by dark green pine trees, and when the photographer developed the pictures, he was shocked by what he saw. A patch of 100 or so larch trees, with their light yellow autumn leaves, stood out from the green pines. They were laid out in the shape of a giant swastika, the reviled symbol of the Nazi party. Once the image got into the press, speculation went into overdrive: who had planted these sinister trees, and when? Their size implied that they must have been planted many years ago, at the height of the Nazi regime. If that was true, it meant that the swastika had been appearing in the forest every autumn for more than 50 years before it was noticed. Possible perpetrators ranged from a Hitler Youth group to a zealous local Nazi official keen to show his support for the Führer, but the mystery was never solved. The authorities made several attempts to remove the trees, but they always regrew.

NAZI BONES

Adolf Hitler's suicide in his bunker as the Red Army marched on Berlin has long been the subject of crazy conspiracy theories. Russian officials have done little to dampen speculation about what happened to his body after his death, and they added to the stories when they unveiled what they believed to be concrete evidence of his demise: parts of Hitler's skull and jaw.

The gruesome find, complete with bullet hole, had been locked away in a vault since the end of the war but was displayed proudly in a Moscow exhibition to mark the anniversary of the war's end. Russian security services would not say how the bones came to be in their possession, but it's rumored that they were picked up as macabre trophies by soldiers of the Soviet Army when they invaded Berlin. The Russian officials enjoyed the irony that Adolf Hitler ordered his body to be burnt before burial, precisely so that his remains couldn't be put on display in Moscow.

THE *TITANIC*

British newspaper editor W. T. Stead had predicted the future. Some years before the *Titanic* set sail, he wrote a story about a steamer that sank in the Atlantic after colliding with another vessel, causing many casualties. Stead predicted that "this is exactly what might take place and will take place if liners are sent to sea short of lifeboats." He also wrote a novel that describes another vessel sinking in the Atlantic; this time the survivors were rescued by an ocean liner of the White Star Line, the company that owned the *Titanic*.

In 1912 Stead was invited by President Taft to speak in America, where he expected to pick up an award, and booked his passage across the Atlantic aboard the *Titanic* on her maiden voyage. When disaster ultimately struck, Stead, one of the most famous Englishmen on the boat, is said to have given away his life jacket and helped women and children on to the lifeboats, whose shortage he had predicted many years earlier. Like many others, he survived the sinking but drowned after clinging to a raft for several hours in the frigid water. Others had more luck—or perhaps not. British engineer John Priest survived the sinking of the *Titanic* in 1912, as well as that of her sister ship *Britannic*, in 1916, and that of the ships *Alcantara* and *Donegal* during World War One. Violet Jessop, a nurse who had survived the sinking of the *Titanic* in 1912, also lived through accidents involving two other White Star Line ships: the collision of the *Olympic* with HMS *Hawke* in 1911 and the sinking of *Britannic* in 1916.

There are other curious coincidences surrounding the tragic sinking of the *Titanic*: being a luxurious state-of-the-art vessel, she had an early movie theatre on board for the upper-class passengers. As the iceberg hit, the theatre was showing an early silent version of *The Poseidon Adventure*, telling the story of an ocean liner, supposedly unsinkable, which was lost at sea.

THE WORLD'S NICEST PIRATE

Not all pirates were murderous rogues who delighted in seeing their prisoners blindfolded and forced to walk the plank. Bartholomew "Black Bart" Roberts, a pirate from Wales, was famous for his discipline and moral fibre. He was a "reluctant pirate," who only turned to the profession after the slave ship on which he was first mate was captured by another buccaneer. He reportedly said that "since he had dipped his hands in muddy water, and must be a pirate, it was better being a commander than a common man." He was teetotal and also a devout Christian, who refused to fight on Sundays and held services for his crew, complete with a band and hymns. Despite capturing vast quantities of the rum beloved by most of his colleagues, he preferred tea, and he enforced a ban on gambling and drinking below decks after 8 p.m. Moreover, he banned fighting between crew members, who weren't even allowed to bring women on board. This didn't stop him being a proper pirate, though, and he pillaged 400 ships of their valuables. In fact, it probably helped.

OLD IRONSIDES

The following tale made the rounds online among patriotic Americans, extolling the virtues of the US Navy and confirming some of the heroic stereotypes regarding the sailor at war. On 27 July 1798 the USS *Constitution*, also known as "Old Ironsides" because of her tough-fought victories under enemy cannon fire, sailed from Boston on a simple mission "to destroy and harass French shipping."

She carried 46,800 gallons of fresh water for her crew of 450: an amount that was deemed sufficient to support six months of operations and military engagement at sea. According to the ship's log she also carried: "7,400 cannon shot, 11,600 pounds of black powder and 71,300 gallons of Kentucky whisky."

Reaching Jamaica on 6 October, she also took on board 400 pounds of salt fish, 800 pounds of flour and 68,500 gallons of rum. A month later she arrived in Dominica, where the quartermaster claimed 500 pounds of beef and 60,000 gallons of local wine. Then she set sail for France.

On the way there she sank six French men-of-war and several cargo ships of the same nationality, salvaging the fine wine they carried aboard. Although her ammunition was exhausted, Old Ironsides made a night raid through the French canals, breaking into a brandy distillery and loading up with 20,000 gallons of cognac in one night. Then she set sail back across the Atlantic.

Seven months later Old Ironsides arrived back in Boston harbor, with no shot, powder, food, brandy, rum, wine or whiskey—and 46,800 gallons of stagnant water. Now that's what they call "sailing the high seas!"

BABY BRIDGE

In nineteenth-century Cornwall, times were hard for farmers, but they needed to have large families, because of the threat of disease and also so that someone would work and take over the farm. One farmer and his wife were expecting their sixth child. Although the expectant mother was excited, the farmer knew that the crops had failed and they could barely afford to support the children they already had.

The months went by and when his wife went into labor, he called for the doctor, who understood the situation and owed him a favor. The two had made a deal: immediately after the birth, the doctor would say that the baby needed medical attention and take it from the house, making sure that it would not survive. The death could then be blamed on natural causes.

It was a long and painful labor, and the farmer couldn't bear to stay in the house. Finally, his wife gave birth to a healthy boy and, as planned, the doctor removed him from her arms, telling her that the child needed to be seen at the hospital. By the time the farmer had returned, the doctor had already disappeared.

He drove out of sight of the farm and dropped the bundle over a bridge, into the river, refusing to tell the father what he had done and only saying that the matter had been settled. The wife never found out what had happened to her child, but the farmer couldn't live with himself and one day took his own life by jumping off that same bridge, leaving his family destitute.

It's said if you stop your car on the bridge and turn the engine off, you can hear a baby crying.

YOU'VE BEEN SHANGHAIED

The Shanghai Tunnels in Portland, Oregon, are some of the most haunted spaces in America. They consist of a complex system of interlocking tunnels running underneath Portland Old Town, connecting the basements of many hotels and bars to the waterfront on the Willamette River. They were originally built to move goods from the docks to the basement storerooms of these establishments, but this wasn't all they were used for.

Enterprising criminals used the tunnels to help fulfil the demand for sailors from the ships that stopped on the West Coast on their way to Asia. There was a severe shortage of young men on these boats, so ruthless gangsters set up operations which would provide them for ships' captains—at a price. The process was known as "crimping" or "shanghaiing," as Shanghai was where many of the victims ended up.

Gangs of crimpers would roam the bars of Portland looking for able-bodied men who had drunk too much or, if they were pushed for time, anybody they could find on the street. If they weren't blind drunk, they were knocked unconscious or drugged, then dragged into basements and dropped into the tunnels through trapdoors. There the unfortunate men would be locked up in subterranean cells until they could be hauled through the tunnels to the docks to start their new career. They were sold to boarding masters who paid as little as $50 per head and took a commission for every man they sourced, so the more bodies the better.

Crimpers would forge the signatures of the captured men who, once on board, were forced to work for no pay. It was actually illegal to leave a ship before it had reached its destination, so any who escaped faced jail. It's thought that thousands of individuals were shanghaied through the Portland tunnels every year and it wasn't just men who were at risk: women were also hauled through the tunnels to be sold into prostitution. They were either kept aboard ships as entertainment for the sailors or sent to foreign cities to work in brothels.

One Portland crimper in particular became legendary. Boarding masters knew that Joseph "Bunko" Kelly would stop at nothing to get them any amount of men they needed. Bunko claimed that he had personally shanghaied more than 2,000 people in a 15-year career that continued until he was imprisoned for murder in 1894. It's said that he once successfully crimped a pair of female prostitutes as sailors for $75 each after drugging them, cutting their hair and dressing them in men's clothes.

Bunko's exploits on another night would go down in history. He was charged with providing 50 men for a British ship bound for China that had docked that day and was leaving the next morning. Bunko was up for the challenge and instructed his men to scour the bars, hotels and brothels of the city, searching for suitable victims. He was walking past a row of saloons, a regular haunt of his, when he heard rowdy voices coming up from the basement and, peering through the doors, saw a room full of drunken men, half-unconscious and groaning. Scattered around them were piles of empty bottles. Bunko soon realized that they were not merely drunk: they had been poisoned. The men, who had been drinking all day together, had been turfed out of one bar so they broke into a cellar, which they thought supplied one of the saloons above, and set to work drinking the place dry. In reality they had found the basement of a mortuary and were guzzling a toxic solution consisting of 90-per-cent-proof alcohol and formaldehyde used for embalming corpses. But Bunko Kelly, ever the professional, didn't let this get in the way of business.

He sent one of his men into the tunnels to get wagons and started sending the incapacitated men down to the docks. The total number varies, according to different accounts, but the haul was at least 25. The boarding master was used to Bunko providing him with semi-comatose sailors, so he thought nothing of it; as far as he was concerned, the crimper had simply fulfilled another contract. The men were dumped into the hold to wait for them to sober up, and the ship set sail with a skeleton crew. But those men never regained consciousness: when the captain went to check on them the next day, they were all dead. It was said that they all looked remarkably good, given all the embalming fluid they had drunk.

The tunnels still exist today, and it's believed that many of the ghosts of shanghaied sailors can be heard groaning down there when ships come into dock.

ELMER McCURDY

One Halloween in the 1970s, a group of kids were spending the day at a California amusement park. They dared each other to go into the house of horrors and then discussed how scary it would be to spend the night there, so they hid away and waited until the park closed.

They larked around the spooky attraction and eventually fell asleep. One of the kids woke up, realized that he was on his own and stumbled around the labyrinth, trying to find his friends and pretending he wasn't scared. Soon he bumped into a body wrapped up like a mummy, which was hanging above him. His stifled scream alerted one of his mates, who crept up behind him and shoved him towards the corpse. The rope holding the figure broke and it fell on the boy, knocking him to the floor, and one of its arms came loose. To their horror the boys realized that it was not a prop, but a real human body—made of real bone and rotten flesh—and in their panic they tore around the attraction in the dark, trying to find the exit.

When they got back to town, they informed the local sheriff, who didn't believe a word of it but decided to pay a visit to the attraction the next day to check out the mummy. When he unwrapped the bandages, he was surprised to see that the face was that of a real dead person, with skin stretched across the bone like old paper and several teeth still in the skull. This truly was a house of horrors.

The operator was immediately suspected as the perpetrator of some grisly crime, but he was mortified, swearing that he knew nothing about the dead body. He had bought it from a touring sideshow operator who had jokingly told him that it was real, but he didn't think for one minute that he had been serious.

The autopsy revealed that the surprisingly well-preserved body was that of a man who had died of bullet wounds at the beginning of the twentieth century. Further investigations revealed his identity as the outlaw Elmer McCurdy, who died in 1911 in a shoot-out with the sheriff after a train robbery went wrong. His last words were the immortal: "You'll never take me alive."

After his death, however, he was taken to a great many places. A mortician embalmed his body after nobody claimed it for burial and put the preserved cadaver on display as a demonstration of his abilities. Elmer's corpse turned into a sort of tourist attraction and he became something of a hero as "the bandit who never gave up." Elmer was eventually released to a man who had pretended to be his long-lost brother and who supposedly wanted to give him a proper burial. In reality he was a sideshow agent and from then on Elmer started a long career in show business.

For more than 50 years his body was displayed at travelling circuses and sideshows, bought and sold a number of times; it was even said that one fairground operator declined to buy him because he wasn't realistic enough. After the kids discovered him hanging in the haunted house, he was finally laid to rest for good. Concrete was poured over his coffin to ensure that he would not be making any more public appearances. Elmer's career as a corpse had been far more successful than anything he ever did while he was alive.

THE TRIBES OF THE SHRUNKEN HEADS

Ever since explorers first ventured into the jungles of South America and brought back tales of cannibals and headhunters, one legend has remained vividly terrifying: the story of tribes that specialise in shrinking human heads. Western adventurers even brought back what they claimed to be genuine heads that had been shrunk to the size of a doll's. Nobody really believed it; they assumed that they were fakes or the heads of monkeys mocked up to look like humans. They were wrong. The practice was widespread and may have carried on well into the twentieth century. The traditional experts at creating shrunken heads, or "tsantsas," as they are known, were the Jivaro tribes of Ecuador and Peru.

The Jivaro people decapitated their enemies and kept their heads as war trophies, shrinking them to the size of an apple, apparently so that their spirits could not reach the afterlife or seek revenge on their killers. They didn't just stop at heads; the Jivaros once killed a Spanish explorer and shrunk his entire body to a height of 3 feet. Foreigners started to buy shrunken heads from the Jivaro in the eighteenth century and this sudden demand kick-started a grisly trade whereby people were killed purely to satisfy the black market.

The common consensus is that head shrinking died out early in the twentieth century as the countries modernised. However, a recently discovered film made by Polish film-makers in the 1960s captured the gruesome process in detail. It shows the Jivaro taking a freshly severed head and slicing the scalp in order to scrape off the skin and hair, yet keeping the face in one piece. This is then boiled in a special mix of plants and bark that contain tannins, like tea, which help to tighten, toughen and preserve the skin—a similar process to the tanning of leather. Any flesh and fat is discarded, and the grisly mask is sewn back together, with the eyelids and mouth sealed, and the head filled with hot rocks and sand. Finally, the head is dried over a fire for around a week to complete the gruesome process. If the videotape is authentic proof that the Jivaro were shrinking heads as late as the 1960s, who's to say they aren't still doing it?

U-BOAT ALERT

In early 2016, online news sites reported that a World War Two Nazi submarine had been discovered in Lake Ontario. The submarine was first noticed by amateur divers a couple of months earlier, although they couldn't tell exactly what it was, as it lay half buried in the sand on the lake bed. They assumed it was a shipwreck, probably an old tourist steamboat, but they couldn't find any mention of it in the guidebooks, so they contacted the authorities. Boats equipped with high-tech sonar imaging equipment were dispatched to the site and revealed its submarine-like shape, so divers from the coastguard were sent down to confirm the findings. The divers descended into the depths of the lake and attached buoyancy tanks to float the mysterious vessel to the surface, where markings still clearly visible on the hull revealed the sinister Nazi connections. But what on earth was it doing in Lake Ontario? Although there had never been any reports of German submarines making it that far inland, German U-boats were known to patrol the Canadian coast during World War Two, and they had sunk several ships off the coast of Newfoundland, including a passenger ferry with more than 100 civilians aboard.

A few years previously, in 2012, local divers in the nearby Churchill River had also discovered what they suspected was a German submarine, but that vessel has never been formally identified or recovered. Suddenly, the intelligence services took an interest. If the two stories were true, there had been a serious lapse in national security. Experts who examined the craft confirmed that it showed all the signs of being a genuine Nazi U-boat.

European officials explained that the boat was an experimental prototype designed specifically for the voyage inland, and that it had been deemed lost off the coast of Canada. They surmised that it had travelled up the St Lawrence River to the Great Lakes, where for some reason it had been unable to complete its mission: to cause panic among the thousands of tourists who travelled to the lake in the summer. If a U-boat could penetrate that far into North America undetected, who knew where they might pop up next? The idea would have struck terror into the hearts of the American public.

The recovered U-boat is to be restored and put on display at a local museum. Experts said that although the vessel has suffered a great deal of corrosion over the decades (and became home to many different fish), it nonetheless fared better at the bottom of the lake than it would have done in a saltwater environment.

LINCOLN AND KENNEDY

Only four Presidents of the United States have been murdered while in office. But that's not all that the two most famous victims, Abraham Lincoln and John F. Kennedy, have in common: the former was elected to Congress in 1846 and the latter exactly 100 years later; Lincoln was elected President in 1860 and Kennedy 100 years later. Both men were fathers who lost one of their children while serving as President, and both were involved with the civil rights movement. Lincoln's secretary was named Kennedy, and vice versa.

When it comes to their assassinations, both were shot in the head on a Friday, with their wives present. Kennedy was shot in a Lincoln car, made by Ford, and Lincoln was shot in Ford's Theatre. John Wilkes Booth, who assassinated Lincoln, and Lee Harvey Oswald, Kennedy's murderer, were born roughly 100 years apart. Both killers had three names composed of 15 characters, and both men were themselves assassinated before trial. Oswald shot Kennedy from a book warehouse, and escaped into a theatre, whereas Booth shot Lincoln in a theatre and ran to a warehouse.

Both Kennedy's and Lincoln's successors were southerners named Johnson. Andrew Johnson, who succeeded Lincoln, was born in 1808, and Lyndon B. Johnson, who succeeded JFK, was born in 1908.

BIG LIZ

In Maryland there is a swamp surrounded by a beautiful landscape with a dark secret. Many years ago the area was covered in plantations worked by slaves. During the Civil War it was rumored that the losing Confederate Army stashed treasure on these plantations, around Chesapeake Bay. It was said that the Union Army recruited slaves who worked on these plantations to feed them information on the enemy and hopefully lead them to the riches that the landowners were hoarding.

Elizabeth was a slave who belonged to a Maryland plantation owner with a particularly murky background, as he was rumored to use his slaves to smuggle money and arms to the Confederate troops in the region. Elizabeth was a favorite of his, because of her sharp mind and loyalty, and he called her Big Liz because of her small stature. As the war wore on and Union troops marched ever closer to his land, her master became worried that he would lose everything, so he enlisted Big Liz to help him bury his gold in the swamp, where nobody would think to look for it. They set off under the cover of darkness with torches, and Liz dutifully dug a deep hole for the treasure under a tree. As soon as she had finished, the slave owner knocked her unconscious and drowned her so that only he knew where his treasure was hidden. But he never emerged from the swampland and some years later his pocket watch was found in the belly of a captured alligator.

When the Union Army came through, and burned the master's house, they reported strange lights floating through the swamp, and one soldier wrote home, describing the disturbing things he had seen. When government agents travelled to the plantation after the war, looking for the treasure, a woman appeared as if from nowhere and told them to follow her, as she knew where they could find it. They never returned.

Big Liz still appears to people who come looking for the treasure, and some say that if you overcome your fear and follow her through the marshes, she will lead you straight to the tree. But nobody ever follows.

TOMMYKNOCKERS

It was 1915 and Arthur was deep in the trenches of northern France during World War One. He was part of a specialist group of troops, all ex-coal miners, whose job it was to dig under the battlefield. The plan was to burrow tunnels under the German trenches, plant explosives and then retreat before the enemy knew they were there. Arthur was an expert and knew exactly how thick the walls of the tunnel should be so that the Germans wouldn't hear them.

One day he was chiselling away at the surfaces when he heard a knocking coming from the other side. He whispered back down the tunnel to see if his mates were responsible for the strange noise, but there was no reply. Then the knocking came again. He hammered at the wall to see if there was a response, but there was silence. When he had clambered back up into the trenches, he told his colleagues what he had heard. Most of them thought it must have been the Germans, digging their own tunnels; they had probably heard Arthur and were just as scared as he was. But one of the miners, an old man from Wales whose breathing had become too labored for him to go down in the tunnels for long, said that when he was mining back home, people used to tell stories about strange noises and voices they heard underground. Some blamed it on the lack of oxygen driving people crazy, but he had once heard them himself. They were called the Tommyknockers, because of the way they would knock on the mines, either to warn of an impending collapse or to bring down tunnels themselves, depending on how the story was told. Arthur laughed, told him to keep his nonsense to himself and went back down the tunnel to continue his digging shift.

Soon he was left on his own again and could tell that he was getting close to the German trenches. He was sure that he could hear voices but couldn't make out what language was being spoken, so he stopped digging to listen. Then came the knocking again, right where he was listening at the wall, and he lay perfectly still. He heard a voice saying in English what sounded like, "Tommy, Tommy," followed by more knocking sounds. He felt a breeze across his face, which carried a voice from beyond the wall, and, very clear this time, he heard, "Get out!" He didn't waste any time in dragging himself backwards through the tunnel, fully aware of the terrible thud of soil falling behind him. He was just about to make it back into the main trench when the earth collapsed around him. He couldn't tell whether he was alive or dead, but the next thing he felt was someone tugging at his feet. He was pulled out into the trench, spitting mud out of his mouth, and saw the face of the old Welsh miner, who shook his head and asked him if he still thought he was full of nonsense. The German trenches had completely collapsed, causing the loss of thousands of enemy troops.

MYSTERIES

THE CRYSTAL SKULL MYSTERY

An aristocratic British archaeologist and his adventurous daughter, Jane, travelled to Central America in the 1920s after hearing stories of mysterious artefacts to be found in the ancient ruins of the natives, who were wiped out by Spanish settlers hundreds of years ago. The pair trekked through the jungle, aided by locals, in search of a lost city full of great riches, possibly Mayan, which had been mentioned in historical documents but never located. Several days into the trip they came across signs of civilization— the remains of a temple in the deep undergrowth—but there was nothing of any value, which might pay for the expedition. Just as her father was ready to give up on the site, Jane tripped over something in the undergrowth that caught her eye: it was a human skull beautifully carved in crystal, which reflected the sunshine of the day so dazzlingly that it was hard to look at it directly. Her father instantly recognized the artefact as one of the legendary skulls, rumored to have mysterious powers, which had been mentioned in books written by Spanish explorers. A loose translation of the Mayan was "skull of doom."

When the locals he had hired saw what the girl was carrying, they were stunned into silence, recognising something of their ancestors that they thought did not exist or would never be found. The story spread fast and the British pair barely escaped with their lives, as every local petty thief knew what was in their possession. Back in Britain, an expert dated the skull as more than 2,000 years old and surmised that the object had been used by priests in sacrificial rituals; it was a harbinger of death.

What made the discovery even more mysterious was the incredible precision of its creation. The explorers took the skull to a state-of-the-art laboratory, where it was analysed, and experts stated that it would have taken hundreds of years to fashion the piece from a single lump of quartz, using diamond tools that could not have been invented 2,000 years ago. This led some to claim that the piece may have had an extraterrestrial origin or was at least the product of lost technology. The creepy artefact went on show in London, attracting admirers from all over the world, and did not take long to exert a strange fascination on all who possessed it.

It was said that mysterious noises emanated from the skull and strange images could be seen in its eyes. Some claimed that the crystal emitted secret coded messages: predictions of doom from the past. Jane, who lived to a great age, swore that the skull had the power of life and death, as the legends had stated. Her father claimed that those who had laughed at the skull's powers dropped dead not long after or became seriously ill. Doctors had told Jane that she had a terminal illness, but she miraculously recovered when the skull was returned to her from an art expert, who reported the piece changing color at random, from black to a bright light. From then on she didn't let the skull out of her sight and refused offers of closer examination.

ZOMBIE NATION

An American anthropologist told the story of a man he met in the Caribbean country of Haiti, an island famous for its voodoo rituals, which are still practised by locals to this day. The young man fell ill with a mysterious malady and was pronounced dead not long afterwards. His family were with him when he died, signed the death certificate and saw him buried. Then they moved on with their lives, until one day—15 years later—somebody claiming to be the dead man appeared in their village. He presented himself to the woman he claimed was his sister, and she could not believe her eyes: it was indeed her brother, back from the dead, and he proceeded to tell her his incredible story. He claimed that their elder brother had sold him to a witch doctor after a family argument over money. The last thing he remembered of his old life was being in the house of the witch doctor, who rubbed a powder made from pufferfish venom onto his skin. This powerful poison, known in medical circles as tetrodotoxin, rendered him paralysed to the point that he appeared dead even to doctors, even though he was in fact still alive. He was completely aware of what was happening to him, but powerless to prevent it. The witch doctors, or "Bokors," of Haiti are said to be experts at using pufferfish poison, fatal even in tiny doses, to bring about a state of reversible paralysis.

Once the man was buried, the witch doctor returned and performed a ritual to bring him back to life, placing him under his spell so that he was only able to do his bidding. The Bokor used drugs to induce a zombie-like stupor, and for several years the man existed in a trance state, working like a slave on a plantation with other victims.

He only managed to break free of the spell when the witch doctor died, and he gained the courage to return to his hometown. His reappearance caused a sensation on the island—surely it couldn't possibly be true?—but many who knew the man before he had "died" testified that he was the same individual. He was able to answer questions about his childhood that only he or his siblings could know. Western anthropologists interested in the voodoo legends also investigated the case and found that he was indeed the same man—and that's not all: he was far from the only case reported by Haitians.

MURDER MYSTERY

During his retirement party, a policeman told his dinner guests about the most intriguing case he had ever worked on as a detective. Although a woman called Suzy Orchard had fallen, or jumped, from the roof of her 20-storey apartment building, she had actually died from a shot to the head. Builders had erected a safety net on the seventh floor, meaning that if it had been a straightforward suicide attempt, it would have most likely been an unsuccessful one. Before she hit the net, however, a shot had been fired through the eighth-floor window, killing her instantly. Did she mean to die? If a person attempts suicide and fails, but is killed by another method, is that still suicide? Or is it murder?

The detective's investigation revealed that an older woman and her husband, who lived on the eighth floor, had been arguing at the time of the incident. The wife had threatened her husband with an old hunting rifle, and in her anger she had fired the weapon, missing him completely and shattering the window. At that exact same moment, Suzy fell past the window into the path of the bullet which killed her. The horrified couple told the detective that the wife regularly brandished the rifle at her husband, but it was never actually loaded. The police were faced with a quandary: were they now dealing with just a bizarre accident? Then another avenue of investigation opened. Some weeks previously a visitor to the old couple's apartment had witnessed their daughter holding the rifle; the detective explained that the father had a strained relationship with her and had recently cut her out of their will. So perhaps the daughter was the one who had loaded the rifle, having seen her mother often threatening to shoot her father with it, in the knowledge that the next time she did so he would be killed. In that case, was she actually a suspect for the murder of Suzy Orchard? That turned out to be closer to the truth, but the charge would not be murder. The daughter *was* Suzy Orchard. She had given up waiting for her mother to kill her father with the loaded hunting rifle and thrown herself off the roof in desperation at her situation.

THE LAST VOYAGE OF THE *LYUBOV ORLOVA*

The *Lyubov Orlova*, a 300-foot-long cruise ship, strengthened to withstand ice floating in the Southern Ocean, was launched in Yugoslavia in 1976. She served as a cruise ship until she ran aground on Deception Island, Antarctica, in 2006. The ship suffered a number of problems and ended up abandoned in Newfoundland after financial wrangling, destined for the scrapheap. She was to be towed by a tug to the Dominican Republic where she could be dismantled but, soon after starting the voyage, the tow line to the tugboat broke, and despite all their efforts, the tug crew could not regain control of the 4,250-ton vessel due to deteriorating weather conditions. The *Lyubov Orlova* was free and started on her lonely journey east across the Atlantic.

The ship turned up in various parts of the ocean, but due to her size and the fact that she was in international waters, nobody wanted to take responsibility. When she turned up off the coast of Ireland several months later, having drifted thousands of miles, it was declared that she might be a danger to shipping, and a warning was issued; even more terrifying was the fact that she might be infested with thousands of diseased rats who survived by eating seabirds and each other. She flashed up on radar, but search planes failed to catch any sight of her. While salvage hunters scoured the waters in the hope of a payday, newspapers warned that she could make landfall at any time with her grisly cargo. The last reports suggested that the ship had missed Ireland but was headed towards the English coast. It was believed that if she ran aground close to shore, thousands of hungry rats would jump ship to find food on land. If the coastguard or salvage hunters found her first, they would have to board her and brave whatever they found below decks. Luckily—or perhaps not—neither the ghost ship nor the cannibal rodents on board have been detected since.

MYSTERIOUS SHOES

A vacationer was walking along the beach on a picturesque island in British Columbia, Canada, when she caught sight of a sports shoe on the sand. There was nobody else around, so she assumed that it must have been washed up by the waves. Upon closer inspection, to her horror, she realized that the shoe contained a human foot in an advanced state of decomposition.

This sight has become a familiar one for beachcombers since 2007, as 16 grisly items of footwear—most of them containing a right foot—have appeared on the shores of Canada and

Washington, with the most recent turning up in February 2016. Where had they come from and to whom did they belong?

Macabre theories emerged: some believed the feet had drifted across the Pacific Ocean for years and belonged to the victims of the 2004 tsunami, while others thought that the shoes' owners were casualties from plane crashes. Another hypothesis was that removing people's feet could have been a local serial killer's or crime syndicate's favorite way of disposing of their victims. Painstaking forensic research identified the former owners of five of the different feet; most of them were thought to be suicidal people who had jumped from bridges in the area and been in the water for some time. But why did people keep finding only their shoes? And why did this happen only in that particular part of the world? The authorities concluded that most of the feet were not deliberately severed, but "disarticulated" after decomposing in the water, and that the kind of shoes people were finding—light trainers and hiking boots—are the sort of items that will eventually float ashore.

HINTERKAIFECK

For several weeks a farmer had been noticing strange goings-on at his property, Hinterkaifeck, where he lived with his wife, daughter and two grandchildren. It was 1922, and the farmer's son-in-law was missing, presumed dead, after serving in World War One. Their maid had recently quit, claiming that the barns were haunted and that she was too scared to go inside.

Early one morning the farmer had seen a mysterious set of footsteps in the snow. They led from the forest to a barn and seemed to end there, so he searched the place carefully, thinking that a tramp may have been looking to escape the cold, but found nobody.

Other things had been happening: the farmer found a mysterious newspaper from another town on his land, while his daughter had reported hearing footsteps in the attic of the farmhouse, where he rarely went, but he dismissed the strange noises as nothing to worry about. Also, a set of keys for the farm had gone missing and although the former maid was a suspect, nothing had come of it. He did not report anything to the authorities—after all, what could they do? But he had mentioned the odd events to neighbors.

A new maid arrived one Friday at the end of March of that year. A few hours later, everybody at the farm was dead: all six people, including the children, had been murdered with a mattock, a heavy tool similar to a pickaxe. The bodies weren't discovered for weeks, until a neighbor came to check on the farm after the mail wasn't picked up and the granddaughter missed school. An investigation of the grisly crime scene led police to believe that the farmer, his wife, the daughter and the granddaughter had been lured out to a barn and murdered one by one. The new maid and the young boy were killed as they slept in the farmhouse. The farmer's granddaughter had been left to die in the barn next to the body of her mother; it was said that she tore her own hair out in distress.

The police suspected a robbery at first, but there was plenty of money still in the house. Bizarrely, despite the farm being unmanned for several days, the animals had been kept fed and watered, and neighbors saw smoke coming from the house over the weekend. More than 100 suspects were questioned over the years, but none were ever charged with the crimes and the farm was demolished the following year. Rumors began spreading amongst locals that the son-in-law may have had something to do with it. His body had never been recovered from the battlefield… so perhaps he wasn't dead after all.

THE POLAR BEARS MADE ME DO IT

A university outside London is housed in a grand old building, renowned for its extensive art collection. At the end of every academic year students take their final exams in a great hall, whose walls are covered with fine paintings. Most students keep their eyes on their exam papers, but some find that the ancient figures watching from inside the picture frames are affecting their performance, and there is one particular image with a terrifying reputation. It's said that if you look at the painting for too long while you sit an exam, bad things will happen. It goes without saying that you will fail the paper, but if the campus legend is true, you could also suffer a far worse fate.

One of the most prized artworks in the university collection is *Man Proposes, God Disposes*, a painting by a famous nineteenth-century artist that depicts the end of a cursed expedition to the Arctic led by an aristocratic English explorer. His ships became stuck in ice and he disappeared with his crew. When rescuers attempted to track them down, they discovered only their frozen bones; the explorers had been reduced to cannibalism in a desperate bid to survive. The painting features two monstrous polar bears tearing at the wreckage of the ship, and one has in its claws the stripped ribcage of a man.

Many years ago a student was struggling with an English Literature exam and scanning the pictures on the walls for inspiration. One of the paintings caught his attention, and he began staring at it, mumbling incoherently. Then, to the horror of the others present, he grabbed a sharpened pencil and shoved it right through his eye into his brain, instantly killing himself. Had something about the painting driven him mad? When shocked tutors read through his exam paper, trying to make sense of his inexplicable actions, they saw that he had scrawled "The Bears!" all over it.

The student's death caused a sensation, and rumors about the painting quickly spread across campus. Soon the fear was so intense that no student would enter the hall during exam season, never mind sit within sight of the polar bears. The college authorities eventually caved to the hysteria and agreed to cover the picture frame with a flag.

Despite his renowned talent, the artist who originally painted the powerful picture was known to have struggled with alcoholism, drug use and depression, suffering a mental breakdown in his thirties. He was eventually declared insane and committed to a mental asylum, where he died within a year. As for the polar bears, they are still hidden from view when exam season comes around.

THE CURSED AMETHYST

Most objects are donated to museums because their owners think the world should see them. Some items, however, are there because the owners want rid of them, as they are cursed and they should not be in any one person's possession.

The Natural History Museum in London has thousands of objects in its collections, all with an interesting story. There is a magnificent display of gemstones, housed in a high-security cabinet known as the vault. If you look carefully in one corner, you will see a purple amethyst stone, decorated with ancient Persian symbols. Although it looks pretty but unremarkable, it is anything but. Its owner once described the amethyst as "trebly accursed and stained with blood and the dishonor of everyone who has ever owned it."

The gemstone first came to the museum in the 1940s, donated by the owner's daughter along with a letter from her father, Edward Heron-Allen, dated 1904 and addressed to "whomever shall be the future possessor." The letter explains that the amethyst was stolen from an ancient Indian temple in the nineteenth century and brought to England by an officer in the Bengal Cavalry who, after taking possession of the stone, lost both health and money. The officer who looted the jewel passed it to his son and he gave it to a friend, who committed suicide and bequeathed the stone back to him in his will. In 1890 he gave the stone to Heron-Allen, a noted London lawyer, naturalist, Persian scholar and spiritualist. He, too, was troubled by various misfortunes until he bound the stone with a metal double-headed snake symbol, with which he claimed to have temporarily calmed the curse.

Heron-Allen kept the amethyst in his library, where both he and his friends saw the ghost of a Hindu holy man thought to be looking for the stone. He lent the jewel to a friend, who was overwhelmed with "every possible disaster" and soon gave it back to him. After more problems, Heron-Allen threw the valuable gem in a canal, hoping to have seen the last of it, but it was dredged up and again returned to its reluctant owner by a knowledgeable dealer. So he gave it to another friend, a singer, who subsequently lost her voice and her career.

When Heron-Allen had a child, he decided to hide the jewel away for good. In 1904, he hid the amethyst inside seven boxes strewn with protective charms and secured it in a bank vault, with the instructions that it should not be removed for 33 years after his death. He included a letter with the jewel, warning any future owners of its powers, with the "advice to him or her to cast it into the sea." Mysteriously, he claimed that he was forbidden to do so himself by an oath to a murky secret society.

Edward Heron-Allen died in 1944, and possession of the stone passed to his daughter, who waited less than a year before donating it to the Natural History Museum. The gem lay there largely unnoticed for decades; it was not on permanent display and the tale of the curse was not publicised. In 2007, though, the jewel was rediscovered and put on public display, along with its incredible story. Soon there were rumblings that the stone had not lost its power. You might think that the highly educated, rational types working in a London museum in the twenty-first century would regard the idea of a "cursed" gemstone as something out of an Indiana Jones film, but the warnings from history continued to echo. The curator responsible for the amethyst display claimed that when he removed it from its case and took it to a meeting of the Heron-Allen society, he encountered a frightening lightning storm on the way there and nearly didn't make it. And that was not all: every time he has removed the stone from the museum, he has been struck down with a mysterious illness, as if the jewel was still intent on bringing misfortune to all who possessed it.

THE NUMBERS STATIONS MYSTERY

Next time you are tuning a radio, keep an ear out for strange voices in the static between the pop music stations. It might be a pirate radio broadcast or perhaps something rather more sinister: mystery transmissions that have been broadcasted intermittently since the start of the Cold War—and nobody knows where they come from, who is sending them or what they mean. Many can be heard on particular shortwave frequencies as a series of buzzes and beeps, possibly Morse code or some other encrypted secret communication. Some "numbers stations," as they have become known, feature robotic voices reading out seemingly random sequences of words or numbers, such as "Yankee, Oscar, Foxtrot," for 24 hours a day.

Some suspect the broadcasts to be messages to undercover agents or sleeper cells waiting for calls to action in foreign countries. Many recognized broadcasts from the number stations have dropped off the radar after the fall of the Soviet Union, but others remain and whether anybody is still taking any notice is the real mystery, as it's possible to track the origin of the messages but much harder to determine who is listening to them. The "Lincolnshire Poacher" broadcast featured a man with an English accent reading groups of numbers separated by the electronic tune of an old English folk song, the "Lincolnshire Poacher." The transmission was heard for decades, suddenly disappearing in 2008. Amateurs are thought to have located the source of the transmission in Cyprus, where the British Air Force has had a presence for many years.

Several people were once charged by United States authorities with the accusation of spying for Cuba; they had allegedly received and decoded secret messages sent via shortwave radio from the communist island. Despite this, no government has ever admitted the existence of the numbers stations. When a radio listener in Europe complained to the BBC that a woman reading out random numbers had interrupted the World Service news, the broadcaster claimed that it was simply a weather forecast for ski resorts. Some have heard regular numbers stations being corrupted or jammed; for example, an English-language numbers station was suddenly interrupted by Chinese music. Nobody knows whether this was a genuine signal for any spies listening, meddling by a foreign power or simply a case of crossed wires.

THE BLOOP

In the late 1990s, the National Oceanic and Atmospheric Administration (NOAA) detected something unusual on their earthquake-monitoring equipment. It was an extremely powerful low-frequency sound rumbling through the ocean, lasting for several minutes, and it seemed to emanate from the middle of the South Pacific, 3,000 miles from land. The sound, which scientists dubbed "the Bloop," was also picked up by the US Navy hydrophone array, usually relied upon to detect Russian nuclear submarines.

The noise registered on their system several times and then disappeared. Nuclear submarines, earthquakes or explosives were ruled out as likely causes. When icebergs "calve" from the ice shelf into the sea, scraping the sea floor, they can cause incredibly loud and long-lasting noises that echo through the ocean, but Antarctic scientists had not recorded any such events. The NOAA have also detected other similar sounds occurring at different locations. For a while the prime suspect was a whale, as the sound profile matched that created by a living creature, but the Bloop was many times louder than even a blue whale, the loudest known creature in the ocean. Is the Bloop the call of an undiscovered monster in the unexplored depths of the deepest ocean on earth?

THE MONEY PIT

There are many islands off the coast of the Nova Scotia peninsula, but one in particular has attracted a lot of attention over the years. Oak Island is around 140 acres in size and is accessible from the shore along a narrow raised causeway built in the twentieth century.

In the late eighteenth century, three young men were exploring the area and decided to investigate the island after seeing lights from the shore. They rowed across the narrow channel from the mainland and started to survey their surroundings. They soon came upon a depression in the land in a clearing amongst the oak trees that covered much of the island. They saw that a rotten and crude pulley system had been constructed over the dip, using an oak tree, and they wondered why. They had all heard the stories about treasure hidden in that area and knew that Nova Scotia, being relatively untouched by Europeans, was a popular haunt of pirates hiding from the British Navy.

There was a legendary pirate called William Kidd, who was hanged by the British in 1701. It was known that before his capture he had buried part of his treasure on an island in the area to use as a bargaining tool. The value of the hoard, and its whereabouts, remained undiscovered after his death, fuelling treasure hunts on several islands. Maybe the boys had chanced upon Kidd's hiding place?

They started to dig and soon hit something hard a few feet below the ground, which turned out to be a layer of rocks. There was nothing underneath but, hoping that something interesting might be buried there, they continued digging and found a layer of logs 10 feet below. And then another. They had excavated a pit dug in the clay soil, with marks made by pickaxes on the walls. It was clearly man-made, but who had dug it, and why?

They managed to dig to a depth of 30 feet, where they found another "floor" of planks, before they had to abandon their search. They hadn't found anything valuable, but they were convinced that something was down there, and others soon caught scent of the treasure hunt. It became known as the Oak Island Money Pit, although no money had been found.

Other treasure seekers, more professional than the boys who had discovered the hole, soon tried their luck. Almost ten years after the original discovery, a company was formed to make a serious excavation of the island. They assembled a workforce and dug far deeper than the boys had managed. They discovered the same marker logs at 10-foot intervals, layers of coconut fibres—a material often used aboard ships to harness cargo—and some kind of putty, possibly used to seal the layers. At the deepest point of their dig, they found something remarkable: a flat stone, similar to the flagstones that had capped the Money Pit, but inscribed with symbols. However, the markings made no sense to anyone in the group, so they recruited linguists to decipher the mysterious runes. Various experts disputed the meaning, but one believed a rough translation to be: "40 feet below, $5 million is buried."

They continued to dig, reaching a depth of almost 100 feet before water started to fill the pit. They claimed to have struck something solid at the bottom, before rising waters forced them to vacate the hole. The next morning, there was too much water to consider going back down so the mysteries of the island had to remain buried for at least another season.

The company returned to the site and dug a new shaft through the clay, under the spot they had reached the last time. They planned to tunnel up into the pit and recover whatever it was that their shovels had struck on the previous dig. All went well at first, but then the cursed hole filled with water and no amount of pumping could clear the tunnel. They had failed. The obvious question was: if they were finding it so hard to even uncover the treasure, how did the original workers manage to bury it and keep it a secret?

Nobody made an attempt on the Money Pit for several decades, but the legend lived on, and digging resumed in the middle of the nineteenth century. Different missions dug several shafts into the pit but all encountered the same problem. They would find intriguing signs, proving that someone had been there before them, but the threat of flooding was ever present. It was too dangerous to deploy men underground, so one firm resorted to using a drill that would drive to the surface whatever it encountered underground. It turned up tantalising clues, including fragments of metal which some supposed were part of treasure chests. Then they felt the drill break through into an air pocket, and they knew that whatever they had found had fallen down into a cavern, whose size was impossible to know. Was this a booby trap designed to stymie even the most determined treasure hunters?

They would not be deterred, though, and poured more money into finding the secrets of the island, even building a dam in the bay to prevent the tide from filling up the hole as it ebbed and flowed. Eventually, this attempt also failed, and the money again ran out. Yet more organizations put up funds for Oak Island hunts, and a drilling operation found another small but intriguing clue: a piece of parchment that was claimed to have Roman numerals written on it. They also maintained to have brought up part of a gold chain, but this has never been verified. All physical clues of this nature have long since been lost.

One expedition even used dynamite to create a crater over the pit, but to no avail. In the early twentieth century another well-funded operation set foot on the island. One of the investors was the explorer and future United States President Franklin Roosevelt, who maintained an interest in the mystery for many years. In the 1930s a businessman bought the part of the island that contained the Money Pit and excavated to a depth of 160 feet, where he found pickaxes, identified as British in origin. It was impossible to know whether these were a clue to the whereabouts of the loot or had been left there by previous treasure hunters who had failed.

Money, pride and reputations were not the only things lost to the pit. In 1861 a man was scalded to death when a steam boiler exploded, and in 1897 a worker was fatally injured after falling into the hole. They would not be the last to perish on Oak Island.

In the 1960s, when the Money Pit treasure was rumored to be worth more than $30 million, a family looking for adventure struck a deal to start another dig and moved to the island. There they lived for years in tough, primitive conditions, with their faith in the existence of the treasure as the only thing keeping them going.

The attempt ended in tragedy when a 30-foot shaft they had dug became filled with toxic fumes which overcame the father of the family. His son attempted to rescue him and he too succumbed, as did two other workers.

Even this did not stop the hunters from coming, though. In 1965 a causeway was built to link the island to the shore, allowing a large crane to dig out a huge amount of earth around the pit. Nothing of any importance was turned up.

In the 1970s an industrial operation plunged steel watertight chambers into the pit and lowered cameras into the darkness. Sensationally, the footage claimed to reveal evidence of wooden chests and human remains, but again this was never confirmed. The island is still a site of great interest to treasure hunters, and investors in various digs have ranged from actors John Wayne and Errol Flynn to the aristocrat William Astor, and even the polar explorer Richard Byrd. However, nobody has ever found any treasure on the island.

Rumors about the treasure and the purpose of the pit have varied wildly: some think that it's not the hoardings of a pirate, but the lost jewels of Marie Antoinette, hidden after the French Revolution, or documents proving that William Shakespeare did not write his plays. Others believe that it's the Holy Grail, planted there by the Knights Templar, a buried Viking ship or an elaborate conspiracy concocted by Freemasons. The mystery of the island will probably never be uncovered, but the hunt is still on.

SURPRISE!

HUMAN PILLARS

An earthquake hit Hokkaido, Japan, in the 1960s and badly damaged buildings and infrastructure. In the aftermath, rescue workers were exploring an old tunnel that had partly collapsed on a railway line. They were looking for survivors or any bodies to recover, but what they found was far more frightening. As they chipped away at the cracked walls, they discovered row upon row of human skeletons in the wall, standing as if to attention, side by side. They must have been there since the tunnel was built, more than 50 years before. They immediately knew what they had found, as stories of "human pillars" had been circulating around the country since the seventeenth century: people who had been sealed inside walls and pillars of buildings either as a punishment or as a cruel form of sacrifice to appease the gods and bless the structure with strength. The practice was thought to have been outlawed centuries ago, but some believed that the grisly tradition had continued for far longer than that. To this day the tunnel is avoided by anybody who knows the story.

WATCH THIS!

A confident lawyer—one of the senior partners—working for a New York law firm was entertaining a group of interns at a party in the skyscraper where the firm's offices were located. He would often joke with the team that the floor-to-ceiling windows in the building were literally "unbreakable," testing their strength as a party piece. Once again, he shocked the students by putting the windows to the test. He ran across the room, launched his body at the glass and bounced right off. Having proved his point, he decided that his audience weren't convinced enough, so he had another go. This time everyone present heard a terrible crack, as the window fell out of its frame, and watched horrified as the lawyer fell with the glass into the street below from the twenty-fourth floor. The firm closed down shortly afterwards.

SECRET STORE

A bizarre news story made the rounds online in 2015, reporting that employees at a Walmart department store got the shock of their lives when they discovered that a homeless couple had been living in a disused storeroom on the top floor of the building for as long as two years. It's not known how the couple came to move into their secret accommodation, but they lived a life of luxury, moving whatever they wanted from the store up to their pied-à-terre, including a king-size bed, television and fridge-freezer. When the items were reported missing, their disappearance was dismissed as petty theft or errors in stocktaking. The pair were only rumbled when they invited homeless friends round for an all-night party at the store, and their guests, somewhat the worse for wear, were caught leaving by staff opening up in the morning.

HOW TO CATCH A BULLET

A magician called Chung Ling Soo wowed his audience by catching bullets fired at his head with his teeth and spitting them out onto a plate. His crowning glory was getting members of the audience to pick bullets for two guns and scratching a personal mark into them. Two assistants then fired at Chung and he would miraculously pick the autographed bullets out of his mouth, totally unharmed, to the shock and delight of his audience.

One night when Chung was performing in London, he chose audience members for the two-gun finale and waited for the weapons to go off. They did and he was shot in the chest at point-blank range. He cried, "I've been shot! Lower the curtain!" and died the day after. The audience were horrified: not only did he not catch the bullet, but Chung was also not supposed to know any English, and he had never before spoken a word onstage. It turned out that he was not Chinese, but an American called Robinson. And he couldn't really catch bullets in his teeth. As his wife explained after his death, the magician had used sleight of hand to swap the marked bullets, which he placed between his teeth, with unmarked ones. The guns that his assistants fired, containing the unmarked bullets, had been modified to direct the flash from the pan to a blank charge. As the guns were never properly fired, they were never properly cleaned, resulting in a build-up of gunpowder. On the night of his death the powder in one rifle caught and the explosion fired the real bullet at Robinson. The mystery was solved, but nobody explained why he put real ammunition in the weapons.

THE TOAST

Everybody who was anybody in town was enjoying the biggest society wedding of the year. The ceremony had gone like clockwork, and the groom was about to give his after-dinner toast. He thanked all the right people, complimented his beautiful wife— as well as her father for putting on such a sumptuous reception and for the very generous honeymoon to the Caribbean—and finally thanked his best man for organising the stag party and for not losing the rings.

The groom announced that he had a special gift for the best man, whom he had known since they were at college together, and gave him a small watch box. When the best man opened it and saw its contents, he turned white, smiled awkwardly at the groom, sat down and polished off a large glass of wine. The groom then thanked all the guests for coming and for the fantastic wedding presents the lucky couple had received. In return he had provided a small token of his appreciation for everyone present, so could they all please check under their chairs?

Taped to the bottom of all the seats was the same picture and a gasp went up simultaneously around the room. It was a photograph of the bride and the best man together. In bed. Nobody knew what to say, but then the groom spoke up again, declaring that he'd had a great dinner and was now off on his honeymoon, alone. It's safe to say that the best man hadn't received a watch.

CRIMES

DUDE, WHERE'S MY CAR?

One day in 1978, a group of children in Los Angeles were digging in their garden, perhaps hoping to strike lucky and find a coin or a piece of discarded jewellery—or maybe an old toy car—when their shovels hit something very big and very hard. When they scraped away the dirt, they saw what appeared to be the unmistakable roof of a car—not quite what they were expecting to find in a suburban garden.

The boys contacted the police, and by the time the authorities had roped off the area and carefully excavated the hole, they realized that it wasn't just the roof: it was the whole car—and not just any car but a 1974 Ferrari Dino 246 GTS, which was in reasonable condition, considering where it had spent the last few years.

It naturally crossed the minds of the investigating officers that this might be an elaborate way of hiding bodies or drugs, but the car was empty. It had been crudely sealed, with sheets and tape on the doors, so the burial seemed to be intentional—but who had left it there, and why? The car, which was estimated to be worth around $20,000 ($70,000 today), still bore the vehicle identification number, which is unusual for thieves to leave intact, so authorities were able to track down the last owner. He had reported it stolen off the street four years earlier, when he and his wife were having dinner in a restaurant. The car wasn't found—for obvious reasons—and he eventually received a large insurance payout. None of the locals in the kids' neighborhood remembered anybody burying a Ferrari at the time, and you would think someone would have noticed it—as one of the investigating officers remarked, "It's not like planting cabbages." The tenants living in the house knew nothing of the buried treasure, nor did the current occupants, who had only moved in a few months previously. Was it an insurance fraud? Had the car owner decided he couldn't afford to run a Ferrari, planted the vehicle underground and claimed the insurance? Or had some thieves come up with an ingenious method of hiding loot from the police?

The recovered car now belonged to the insurers, who put it up for auction at less than half its value. It was bought and eventually restored by a mechanic, who finished the car with the registration "DUG UP." Similar vehicles today are worth upwards of $400,000. So why was the car buried? The rumor was that the owner hired a couple of career criminals to steal the Ferrari, asking them to dump it in the ocean so he could collect the insurance premium. When the crooks saw what they had on their hands, however, they decided to keep it for themselves, hiding the car underneath the yard of an unsuspecting householder and planning to come back for it one day. The thieves were never caught, but it's nice to imagine that they eventually returned with shovels to the spot, only to find it gone.

BONNIE AND CLYDE

Legendary bank robber Clyde Barrow, of "Bonnie and Clyde" fame, was known for two things: his ruthlessness and his uncanny ability to evade the police after jacking a joint. He was a getaway car connoisseur; it helped to have the best vehicle available at your disposal when you needed to outrun the law. Historians recently unearthed a letter from Clyde to motor car pioneer Henry Ford, in which he proclaims his love for the Ford V8—his stolen getaway vehicle of choice, where he and his accomplice would eventually die in a hail of bullets. The letter states that Barrow always drove Fords, at least when he was able to get his hands on one for a job. The letter says,

> While I still have got breath in my lungs, I will tell you what a dandy car you make [...] For sustained speed and freedom from trouble the Ford has got ever [sic] other car skinned and even if my business hasn't been strictly legal it don't hurt anything [sic] to tell you what a fine car you got in the V8.
> Yours truly, Clyde Champion Barrow.

The motoring magnate received the message only a month before the shoot-out.

THE DARK WEB

Even outwardly normal and intelligent people can be seduced by the dark side of cyberspace. In 2004 British police received an emergency call from a teenager who had been attacked in a city alley. He spent a week in critical condition in hospital and, despite receiving serious stab wounds to internal organs, he managed to survive. The boy told the police that an older man dressed in black had committed the crime, unprovoked, and was even able to give a detailed description, so an appeal was broadcast on the news for any witnesses to come forward.

When the police studied surveillance camera footage of the alley, however, they realized that the case was a lot more complex than it had first appeared—it would lead them into "the dark side of the internet." The camera captured the victim on the scene, but with him was another teenage boy, whom he hadn't mentioned to the police. There was no sign of the alleged man in black. After the victim was confronted with the evidence, he said that the other boy had attacked him in the alley, but he didn't know why. The story didn't make sense, until detectives searching through the boy's computers uncovered the fact that the two had met previously in an internet chat room. After trawling through thousands of messages between the pair, police gradually unravelled the bizarre case.

The victim, known as Jack, as he was too young to be publicly identified, had spent half a year ensnaring Max in an elaborate deceit. Jack pretended to be several different characters in the chat room to fool Max into doing what he wanted. He initially pretended to be a girl, who introduced Max to her "brother," who was actually Jack himself. He then created other fictional characters, including a girlfriend and secret service agents inspired by James Bond films. Police eventually linked all the false identities to Jack because they all made the same spelling mistakes in the chat room.

Max, who was convinced that the characters were real and that Jack was dying of an incurable illness, was persuaded by a fake female secret service agent to do what she ordered in order to serve the British intelligence services. He believed that if he passed the test, he would be entrusted with a firearm, meet the British Prime Minister and receive a large amount of cash. Max's big test, if he wanted to be a spy, was to murder Jack. "It was incitement to commit murder—his own murder," said the policeman in charge of the investigation.

On the day in question, Max travelled to Jack's hometown and carried out the attack, believing that he was working for the British secret service. He was convicted of attempted murder and Jack was charged with inciting his own murder—the first ever such charge. Neither boy was jailed. The judge summed up the affair: "Skilled writers of fiction would struggle to conjure up a plot such as that which arises here."

SERIAL SCOOP

Citizens of Macedonia became transfixed by a series of grisly murders of elderly women from the same town. Police suspected the crimes to be the work of a determined and thorough sadistic serial killer. Worried members of the public turned to the pages of a small local paper for the latest details, as it always had the juiciest information on the terrible crimes. The reporter on the story, a seasoned crime journalist with over 20 years' experience on the job, seemed to have a fascinating insight into the mind of the killer. With each murder, and each report in the paper, the police began to become suspicious. They wondered who the reporter's source was and thought there might be a leak in the investigation. The information he was revealing had never been released to the public so did that mean that he was in communication with the murderer? None of the other journalists covering the story knew, for example, that the murderer had used a telephone wire to strangle his victims.

Then, in an incredible scoop, the paper revealed where one of the bodies might be buried and when the police checked it out, the location turned out to be correct. And it wasn't long before another body was discovered thanks to the investigative reporter. Then police made a breakthrough of their own and arrested the reporter on suspicion of committing the murders. They discovered that DNA evidence linked him to the victims, who all knew his mother and looked like her, too. The journalist was charged with two murders, and suspected of two others, but he killed himself in custody before he could be put on trial, taking the final story to the grave.

IN THE FIRING LINE

A story concerning a pair of poachers who had been picked up by police appeared in a local Scottish paper. The officers were alerted after the suspects crashed their truck on a remote estate in the mountains. After talking to the men, the police ascertained that they had been travelling back to their village following a successful hunt late at night, when the truck's headlights had failed and they couldn't continue. They tracked the problem down to the fuse box near the steering wheel and one of the men remembered hearing in the pub that you could use a .22 calibre bullet as a temporary fuse, so he removed one from his rifle and placed it in the box. The headlights came back on and they continued their journey. Just before they pulled onto a notoriously dangerous pass that sloped away down into a deep valley, they heard a loud bang and the driver cried out in pain, just as the truck veered off the road and crashed into a tree. The improvised fuse had overheated and exploded, firing straight into the poacher's groin. They were promptly arrested and, despite one of them needing to undergo a rather sensitive surgical procedure, the poachers were relieved: if the bullet had exploded when they were on the mountain pass, they might not have survived at all.

WHODUNNIT?

A French crime writer finished his latest book and sent it to his publisher, who read it with horror. It was a thriller that explored seven ways in which the narrator might have killed his wife. A disturbing topic—and given that the writer's real-life wife had disappeared without trace a year before, it was particularly shocking. The author had been the prime suspect in the disappearance, but police had dropped the charges due to lack of evidence—and lack of a body.

The publisher rejected the manuscript as too unpleasant—in one of the fictional deaths the body was put through a meat grinder—and then forgot about it. But rumors surrounding the book's existence began to leak out, and the writer seemed to revel in them. He even commented to neighbors that a hole he was digging in his garden was big enough for a body—but still no body had been found. When asked about his wife by interested journalists, he made cryptic comments that did nothing to dampen suspicion of his guilt, but eventually he remarried and moved to a different city.

The writer was finally arrested after the family who moved into his old house dug up the garden and found a human skeleton buried under a shed, later identified as his missing wife. He confessed to killing her and was jailed. He had beaten her to death, buried her under concrete and reported her missing. He never explained why he killed her, nor why he wrote the gruesome book that threatened to expose his crime, which has yet to see the light of day.

TRUE CRIME

In the year 2000 a businessman was abducted, tortured and murdered in a Polish city. His body was found in a river, and investigators discovered that he had been bound and strangled. The police had few leads to go on and the trail eventually ran cold. The case was closed and filed away as "unsolved" for several years, until one of the investigating officers read a violent thriller by a local crime writer, whose plot he found very interesting indeed. In the book a woman is abducted, tortured and killed in a manner identical to the 2000 murder—and what's more, the perpetrator gets away with it.

The author was questioned but released without charge on lack of evidence, as he claimed that he had read about the case in the papers at the time and merely thought it would make for a good story. However, the veteran policeman was still suspicious; he had uncovered the fact that the writer, known to be a jealous and extremely controlling man, had an ex-wife who had been in a relationship with the man found in the river. Although it was never proved that he committed the crime, the court noted that the villain in his book bore a strong resemblance to his creator and ruled that the writer must have been involved in the original murder. Almost ten years after the crime, he was sentenced to life imprisonment. The authorities are keeping their guard up, however, as the killer author is said to be working on a second volume in prison.

CARPET PEOPLE

Why do people in movies put bodies in carpets? Isn't that a little impractical? Do bodies really get rolled up in spare rugs? In the 1980s, three college students in New York were walking back to their apartment on the West Side of Manhattan when they noticed a carpet rolled up on the pavement and promptly carried it home. It's not known why they did this, but they were students after all. They commented on how heavy it was, and one said that it probably meant that it was good quality. When they got the item back to their apartment and unrolled it, they were surprised to find a dead body inside: a man who had been shot in the head. "They thought they were going to decorate their little dorm room," explained a policeman who was investigating the grisly find. They probably lost their enthusiasm for interior design pretty quickly after that.

HUMAN HARVEST

A gang of sadistic criminals, who seemed to be killing at random, terrified the population in a remote region of Peru in 2009. Locals had not forgotten tales of the "Pishtacos": ancient demons that would kill people and eat their body fat.

The gang would lie in wait for passers-by on lonely roads, lure them into the rainforest with promises of work and then kill them. If this wasn't scary enough, the police investigation revealed that these modern devils really were pishtacos, as they were harvesting their victim's body fat to sell in the country's capital for use in skin cosmetics. The authorities believed that they had been active for years and may have killed more than 60 people to keep their macabre business afloat. The gang's method was to dismember their victims, hang their torsos from hooks and slowly cook them until the fat dripped into tubs. When the police finally arrested them, they were found to be in possession of several bottles of liquidised human lard, which fetches high prices on the international black market.

MAFIA TV

Italian authorities have recently revealed that the country's powerful Mafia clans hijacked a popular football television show in order to send encrypted messages to their associates in prison. The messages went undetected for months and even reached gangsters who were kept in isolation, supposedly so as to stop them communicating with their accomplices.

Criminals who appeared to be watching the latest football scores on TV were actually keeping up to date on Mafia news by reading text messages sent in to the show by viewers. The messages, disguised as comments from fans, scrolled along the bottom of the screen but the show's producers were none the wiser and did not know about their specialist audience. The ruse was only discovered when the authorities intercepted a letter to a jailed godfather, in which his underlings suggested that he watch the football show.

Incarcerated Italian Mafiosi have always dreamt up creative ways of bypassing authorities in order to send messages to the outside world. One jailed boss received information about his trial over the radio from underlings who requested songs with particular meanings. A Naples mob went further and bought an entire radio station so that they could broadcast song requests with dedications that contained coded messages for their colleagues in jail and on the run.

DRUG MONEY

Colombian drug lord Pablo Escobar once supplied an estimated 80 per cent of all the cocaine used in the United States. This made him a large amount of money, and most of it in cold hard cash, which led to some logistical problems. It was said that his $20 billion empire required him to spend $50,000 per year just on rubber bands to wrap around the bills, and his operation budgeted to lose around 10 per cent of its profits each year because rats would always eat some of the money while it was stashed in warehouses. He even bought a private jet purely to transport cash back to Colombia. When the net finally closed around Escobar, he didn't change his relaxed attitude to cash: after being forced to go on the run with his family, he literally burned through $2 million in cash just to keep them warm at night. Even now, 20 years after his death, it's believed that there are millions of dollar bills still buried in the Colombian jungle and in the walls of the various properties he owned, waiting to be found—if the rats haven't got there first.

THE RELUCTANT ROBBER

The police had never seen a stranger bank robbery. A middle-aged pizza deliveryman with no previous convictions had walked into a bank with a home-made shotgun disguised as a walking stick and demanded hundreds of thousands of dollars. The bank teller handed over $10,000 and the robber left but was intercepted by police, who noticed that he had a strange metal collar around his neck. He claimed it was a bomb. According to the man's story, he had been kidnapped by three men who had fixed the explosive around his neck and forced him to rob the bank. If he refused to do their bidding or deviated from the plan, the bomb would be remotely detonated.

The police didn't believe him at first and, assuming it was an elaborate hoax, they attempted to apprehend the suspect. But it wasn't a trick; the bomb exploded and killed the robber before the police had a chance to rescue him. It was later revealed that the device was rigged to explode if tampered with. The police found a note on his body containing instructions he was to carry out to complete the robbery before the timer on the bomb went off. The cops worked out that it would have been impossible to finish all those tasks in time: the bomb was always going to explode. The investigating officers had no idea whether to believe the robber or not: was he an innocent victim driven to desperate measures or was he in on the job? Was he perhaps tricked by his accomplices into thinking that the bomb was a fake?

Federal prosecutors were baffled, and nobody was charged with the crimes until several years later, when two of the supposed kidnappers received life sentences for "using a destructive device in a crime of violence" and the conspiracy to rob the bank. A third co-conspirator, who some suspected of being the bomb-maker and ringleader, died before he could be arrested, whereas a fourth accomplice walked free after making a deal with prosecutors. The actual robber's part in the scheme was still unclear. Although the authorities insisted that the pizza deliveryman was part of the gang, they believed that he did not know the bomb was real and that when he realized the seriousness of the situation, it was too late for him to back out. The man's family still refute all allegations that he was a willing participant in the crime, insisting that he was an innocent victim of a cruel plot.

SLEEPER TRAIN

An American student was travelling across Europe by train for his summer vacation. He had passed through France and Germany, and one night he was on his way over the Italian border from Switzerland. He was excited about this next part of the trip, and planned to see all the major Italian cities and visit the village where *The Godfather* movie had been filmed. He was still a long way from his next stop, however, so he settled down for the night in his single cabin, as the train wound its way through the mountains.

When he woke up, he was surprised to find that it was early evening, and people were walking past his cabin to the restaurant carriage. He had slept for nearly an entire day and felt terrible. It was as if he had the worst hangover ever, but he had drunk only one glass of wine the previous night—maybe there had been something wrong with the food? Had he been drugged? He patted himself down and was relieved to find that his money belt was still round his waist; he quickly checked his belongings and they were all there. The cabin door was locked, so nobody could have entered, but the window was wide open, even though he thought he had closed it the previous night. He walked slowly down the train to the restaurant car to get a cup of coffee, wondering what had happened, his thoughts still slow in coming. He finished the drink and fished around in his money belt for his wallet to pay for it. To his horror, he was only carrying a few coins. He was positive that there had been several hundred euros in there when he had fallen asleep. He stumbled back to his cabin in a panic, but the money was nowhere to be found. He had been robbed—but how? To get to the cash the thieves would have had to pull him out of bed, undress him and remove the money belt, all without waking him.

He set off down the carriage again, found the train guard and explained to him in broken Italian that somebody had stolen his money. Luckily, the guard spoke English and followed him to his cabin, where he conducted a brief search and asked him whether he had opened the window, as the train had made unscheduled stops during the night, so perhaps someone could have entered through there. When the student questioned how anybody could have entered the train, committed such a robbery without waking him and then exited through the window before the train left the platform, the guard ignored him, asking instead how many drinks he had consumed the previous evening. As the student insisted that he hadn't been drunk and started to request that the other passengers be searched, the guard told him to get off at the next stop and ask the police for help, as he didn't have the necessary authority. Realising that he wasn't going to get anywhere with the guard, the student resigned himself to a miserable few hours of worry in his cabin until the train arrived at the next stop: a small town in the Alps.

When they arrived, the guard told him that they had a maximum waiting time of 30 minutes—any longer and they would have to leave him behind. The student found the small police station near the station and explained the situation to the English-speaking policeman on duty, who listened and nodded patiently, as if already familiar with the events. He then explained to the American what had probably happened: he had been a victim of specialist train robbers. They pounced at night, when passengers were likely to be asleep, but they made sure that their victims didn't wake up by spraying sleeping gas under the cabin door. Then they donned gas masks and entered the room with a regular key, either stolen from the guard or obtained with bribes. The policeman explained that train staff often colluded with the criminals in return for a cut of the proceeds (now the train guard's unhelpful attitude made sense!). When the thieves found what they were looking for, they opened the cabin windows to let out the sleeping gas and disembarked at the next stop, hours before their victim even regained consciousness. The policeman explained that he would do what he could, but the unfortunate American was unlikely to see his cash again. Resigned, the student suddenly realized that he was running out of time and only had ten minutes to get back to the train, so he thanked the officer as he ran out of the door and arrived back on the platform in plenty of time. But the train was nowhere to be seen; it had left without him, with all his luggage on board.

ANOTHER RELUCTANT BANK ROBBER

A New York motorcycle courier was riding to his next pick-up at a bank downtown that he hadn't visited before. The instructions said that, because the clients had a deadline to meet, there was no time to spare and he didn't need to go inside. Instead, there would be a man waiting out front with the package. The pick-up went as planned, and a man on the pavement outside the bank handed him a heavy bag and hurried off. The motorcyclist sped off on one of his favored routes through the back alleys and shortcuts of the city, knowing that nobody could cover the route as fast as he could.

He arrived at his destination in double-quick time and was too busy congratulating himself on his personal record to notice that it was a strange place for a drop-off from a bank: an abandoned building by the docks. As he stepped off his bike, he heard the sound of sirens and soon was surrounded by police officers. He protested that he hadn't broken any speed limits, but the officers grabbed the bag from his shoulders, tore it open and hundreds of $50 bills burst out onto the street. The courier had become a bank robber without realising it.

NEIGHBORHOOD WATCH

Have you ever wondered whether your neighbors are up to something? Digging the garden late at night? Asking you to move suspiciously heavy rugs? In 1984 a man was asked by his neighbor, a young woman, to help her lift some heavy, old carpet roll out of her basement. He didn't think much of it; he noted that it was old and bulky, but merely assumed that it might contain several carpets rolled up together. The woman also enlisted the help of her three young children to help lug the rug onto the landing, where she told the helpful neighbor that she would take care of it from there. She was later convicted of her husband's murder, although she claimed that she had actually shot him in the head by accident. She had hidden the body in a roll of carpet in the basement before burying him in a shallow grave in the backyard.

The kind neighbor told reporters that he used to carry out favors regularly for others living nearby, but that he would no longer do so: "I don't carry no more carpets."

DEATH

ROAD TO HEAVEN

Sandra Ilene West, the glamorous ex-model wife of a late Texan oil magnate, lived the high life in Los Angeles. She was reportedly a keen student of Egyptology, and the ancient Egyptian concept of being buried with one's most prized possessions apparently appealed to her. In 1977, when she was only in her thirties, she was found dead of mysterious causes in her Beverly Hills mansion and it quickly became clear that she had been determined to continue her luxury lifestyle into the afterlife. Her relatives were surprised—or perhaps not—to learn that she had left instructions that she should be buried next to her husband, wearing a lace nightgown and sitting in her favorite Ferrari—she had several—with the "seat slanted comfortably." Her brother-in-law, who stood to receive $2,000,000 from the estate if her wish was carried out, nonetheless went to court to avoid the elaborate funeral. After weeks of deliberation, the judge eventually ruled that there was no legal reason why someone should not be buried inside a Ferrari and that Sandra should finally be laid to rest according to her wishes. When the day came, her body was flown to Texas, wearing a nightgown, and was placed in her powder blue 1964 Ferrari 250 GT, today worth millions, with the seat comfortably reclined. The car was then loaded inside a container, lowered into a 9-foot-deep hole and covered in concrete to deter grave robbers. The simple gravestone beside her husband's provides no hint as to her luxurious resting place below.

SWEET KISS OF DEATH

An American jockey was riding the 20-to-1-shot horse, Sweet Kiss, in a 2-mile race in New York City when he slumped over in the saddle, somehow managing to stay on board as his horse went on to jump the last fence and cross the line in first place by a head. He didn't celebrate his win—the first of his career—as, when the horse's owner went to congratulate him on the race, he found him dead. He had suffered a heart attack during the race, becoming the first and only corpse to win a horse race in the United States. It was thought that the attack had been brought on by the strict weight loss regime undertaken by the horse trainer—he was not a regular jockey—and the excitement of riding a winner.

THAT'S NOT FUNNY

It was the week before Halloween, and towns across America were being decorated with pumpkins, witches' hats and spider's webs, ready for the parties to come. Some householders went further than others, hanging skeletons from windows and even hoisting dummies mocked up as corpses on trees and garages, or protruding from car boots. Some locals complained that such decorations were tasteless and brought the neighborhood down, while some were even scared enough to call the police. A few days before Halloween, a frightening figure appeared overnight hanging from a tree near a busy road, but most of the people who drove past weren't that shocked, and nobody made any calls to 911—not for a couple of days at least.

Then somebody walking past the decoration thought that it looked a little too realistic up close and, upon closer inspection, discovered why: it was the real dead body of a woman who had hanged herself.

Similarly, in another town a man had shot himself in the head on his balcony and lay undisturbed for several days after his neighbors mistook his lifeless body for an elaborate Halloween decoration. More recently, people in an Ohio neighborhood were shocked when construction workers realized that a dummy hanging on a fence was not, as they had assumed, a stupid Halloween prank, but the body of a murdered woman. So next time you see a gruesome Halloween set-up, you might want to check whether it's real...or maybe you don't...

WAKE-UP CALL

Early morning phone calls can be such a pain! One Saturday in 1992 a middle-aged North Carolina man was woken early by the sound of his telephone ringing on his bedside table. Still half asleep, he reached for the phone but grabbed instead the Smith & Wesson .38 handgun he had left on the table the night before. Much to the horror of his wife, who was watching from the other side of the bed, he put the revolver to his head, as if answering a call, and the gun discharged, killing him instantly.

THE ELECTRIC CHAIR

A convicted murderer spent several years in solitary on death row, bound for the electric chair, until at the last moment his lawyers managed to get his sentence commuted to life. Some years afterwards he claimed to have turned his life around and to have dedicated himself to his studies. He was still kept in solitary, where inmates were allowed a small TV set to keep them company, provided that they used headphones. One night the reformed man was sitting naked on the metal toilet in his cell, trying to fix the earphones that enabled him to hear the television, when he accidentally bit into a live wire and dropped down dead from electrocution. He had been killed by an electric chair of his own making; perhaps a little more studying had been required.

WAKEY-WAKEY

An electronics student from China had reluctantly travelled to the United States to continue his education. He was there at the behest of his family, who had sacrificed much to send him and expected him to be a success. There was one major stumbling block, though: he always had trouble getting up on time. He had tried everything, from drugs to hypnosis and alarm clocks, but he was still missing lectures, and back home his family were wondering why his grades were not up to scratch.

One day he saw an advert for an alarm clock that gave small electrical shocks to wake people up and, as he was desperate for something that could get him out of bed in the morning, he decided to look into it. He couldn't afford the item in the advert, so he decided to use his skills to build it himself, also proving to himself and his family in the process that he wasn't useless. He began by borrowing some lecture notes from his classmate, who never missed a lesson, on how to construct the required circuits. He then collected a car battery, clock and wires, and worked through the night to put the contraption together, adding the final touches by attaching himself to the device and setting the alarm to wake him in plenty of time for his early-morning lecture. Satisfied with his work, he slept easily.

He never woke up. Later that morning his classmate came to his room to retrieve her borrowed lecture notes. She assumed that he was asleep, as usual, but then she noticed the contraption and the burn marks around his head. She found no pulse and, horrified, she saw her notes still out on the desk. The college investigation found that the sleepy student had miscalculated terribly and the car battery had shocked his heart with a lethal current, killing him instantly.

MUMMY DEAREST

A terminally ill taxi driver from England found fame beyond the grave after responding to a newspaper advert looking for volunteers to be mummified in the style of the ancient Egyptians. The researchers wanted to see how effective the process really was, and he thought it would give his grandchildren something special to remember him by. When the man's time came, his body was handled according to the 3,000-year-old technique used to preserve the corpse of Pharaoh Tutankhamun: his organs were removed, leaving only the brain and heart, and sealed in jars. Then his insides were cleaned out with alcohol, packed with bags of spices and sawdust, and stitched back up again. His body was soaked in salt water for several months, and his skin treated with oil and wax. Finally, his corpse was wrapped in linen sheets and left to dry for three months. The experiment was judged to be 100 per cent successful, yielding results regarded as extremely authentic. The modern mummy was then taken to its final resting place at a medical museum in London, where it can be studied by archaeologists used to examining rather older specimens.

FAN DEATH

Some people believe that if you leave an electric fan running in the room where you sleep, you will never wake up. The stories first originated in Asia, particularly in South Korea, where it was said that the technology could suck the life out of unsuspecting people as they slept. Explanations ranged from asphyxiation, caused by the fan displacing oxygen from the room, to hypothermia, as the contraption drives heat away from the body. Some say that the rumor was started by a government official in a bid to reduce electricity consumption. Fans sold in parts of Asia now have timers to ensure that they turn themselves off after a set period of time, but whatever the truth, South Koreans still remember to turn them off before falling asleep, just to make sure.

THE DEAD PHONE LINE

A high school student called Dave, who was planning to attend a top military academy, had been found dead in his room. He was in peak condition, as attested by the physical exam that he had recently passed with flying colors. Relatives found him in his bedroom, a telephone still next to his ear, as if he had died before he could end a conversation. He had only been alone in the room for a few minutes and the person who had been on the other end of the phone line described hearing only a click and then a short gasp. '

It was months before investigators found the cause of death. A post-mortem revealed no external injuries, but forensic scientists discovered that he had died of bleeding in the inner ear, thus indicating some kind of electrical surge that had shocked the brain via the auditory nerve. Experts suspected that the phone held the clue. There had been a powerful thunderstorm on the night when Dave died, and they thought that lightning could have struck the phone cables and passed a fatal shock through the receiver. But there was no physical evidence in the boy's room to suggest that this had happened, not even any burns on the phone line.

In the end, it was concluded that the only possibility was that the phone had killed him. Investigators working on the case discovered that a lightning strike can give you a fatal electric shock though a phone line without leaving any evidence of burns or damage on the phone line itself. The electricity passes straight into your inner ear, and from there to your brain, without the usual resistance provided by the body. Therefore, it's probably best to avoid using your phone during a thunderstorm.

I BELIEVE I CAN FLY

Way out in the Arizona desert, a police patrol looking for a missing man from a nearby town came upon what looked like a car wreck, but this was no normal accident. The vehicle was stuck impossibly high up the side of a cliff, at least 100 feet above the road below. It took weeks for accident investigators to sift through the evidence and work out what had happened. After inspecting every bit of the wreckage, they eventually found fragments of a driving licence and realized that they had found their missing man.

The ex-air force engineer, who had always wanted to be a pilot, had got hold of a miniature jet engine from the base where he used to work and attached it to the back of his family saloon car. His goal was to take it to the Utah Salt Flats and break a land speed record. First of all, though, he needed to test the system, so he headed out into the desert to see what speed he could get up to. As dawn broke, he pointed the car down an empty straight road, estimating that he had about 5 miles of straight tarmac before he needed to brake. He started the car rolling with the conventional engine, reaching the speed limit, and then ignited the jet. At first there was no difference, but then he heard the turbine winding up and he was shoved back into his seat by the acceleration, unable to lean forward and turn off the ignition. He covered those 5 miles in no time at all, and then the flat road gave way to a canyon. The car destroyed the traffic barrier and flew right over the ravine, crashing into the other side. At the man's funeral, his friends remarked grimly that at least he had died following his dream.

YOUR WORST NIGHTMARE

A middle-aged woman from Kazan, Russia, was rushed to the local hospital by her husband after collapsing at her home. She had suffered a suspected heart attack and was declared dead on arrival. The funeral was arranged for a couple of days later and the coffin put on display. The relatives had arrived and the ceremony had begun, when they heard a knocking sound coming from somewhere in the funeral parlor. They all looked at each other, and when the screaming started, they soon realized where it was coming from: inside the coffin. The woman was not dead, and she had awoken in the middle of her own funeral. Any relief her relatives might have felt after the terrible shock had worn off soon reverted to sadness, as the supposedly deceased was so traumatised by the experience of hearing her loved ones praying for her that she suffered a second heart attack at the scene, which really did kill her...At least her incompetent doctors hoped it had.

THE CRATER

In the Godzilla stories, Mount Mihara, a volcano on the Japanese island of Izu Oshima, is where the government imprisoned the famous monster. In real life, it is an equally frightening place. The volcano is active, and from a rocky outcrop you can see the boiling crater and clouds of sulphur. In the 1920s an unhappy schoolgirl hiked up to the viewing spot and committed suicide by jumping into the crater. A few weeks later another girl heard about the incident and followed suit. The suicides were all over the news, and before long it became a popular place for people to take their own lives in a spectacular fashion, the idea of instant cremation catching people's imagination. Hundreds of macabre sightseers flocked to the island—many of them booking one-way tickets—and it was not unusual for at least one person every day to throw themselves into the lava. The volcano continued to take lives until the 1930s, when more than 600 people committed suicide there in one year alone. The pull of the island proved so strong that the government stepped in and barred entry to the jumping spot, stopping the sale of one-way tickets and leaving the volcano alone to wait for its next eruption.

SCREAMATHON

It was once the tradition at a California university to organise "screamathons" in the dormitories. Everybody in on the joke—sometimes hundreds of students—would holler at the top of their voices at a designated time, usually midnight or the early hours, for no apparent reason other than to blow off steam in exam season or terrorise unsuspecting classmates and supervisors. The practice happened once or twice a term and had been going on for years. One night, when another screamathon was due to take place, the dormitory suddenly erupted in a cacophony of screaming and howling for 30 seconds, right on schedule at 1 a.m., before everything went quiet again.

The next morning a girl was found dead in her room. Investigators estimated the time of death to be between midnight and 2 a.m., but fellow students knew exactly when she had died: she had been strangled at exactly 1 a.m., when nobody could hear her scream. That was the last screamathon at the university. The perpetrator was never found, so nobody knew whether it was a student who was in on the joke or an intruder who had slipped in and out without anybody noticing.

THE STAG PARTY FROM HELL

A newly engaged man from Minnesota had big plans for his stag party. He and his friends were going to hire a motor home and drive more than 800 miles across four states to the Kentucky Derby in Louisville. They picked out their party ride and went on the road. After only a couple of hours, his mates started to complain about an unpleasant odor in the vehicle.

They thought it might be coming from outside, but closing the windows didn't help, so they turned off the air conditioning to see if that was the culprit, but it made no difference. They had to stop off for supplies, so they took the opportunity to search the vehicle from top to bottom, looking for the source of the terrible stench. They soon found it. One of the men opened a luggage compartment in the body of the motor home and almost passed out: there was a corpse stuffed inside, and it wasn't fresh. Immediately, the men's thoughts turned to the person from whom they had rented the van, who had told them specifically that the front luggage holds were not working and were not to be opened. The stag party were held up for several hours as police questioned them. They never made it to the horse race.

WATER WAY TO GO

A group of forestry workers were trudging through the blackened remains of a thousand-acre California forest that had been destroyed by a recent fire. As they assessed the damage— stepping over the still smouldering, barren landscape and avoiding the bodies of the small mammals that hadn't managed to escape the smoke—they came upon something both shocking and utterly puzzling: the charred remains of a man unmistakably dressed as a diver, complete with melted flippers, wetsuit and oxygen tank, which was still intact despite the fire.

When the authorities tried to identify the unfortunate man, they unravelled an unbelievable tragedy. First of all, the post-mortem revealed that the diver did not die from burns or smoke inhalation, but from head and internal injuries. Then the mystery deepened, as it transpired that on the day the fire took hold, he had been diving in a regular spot near a wreck off the coast, some 30 miles away from where he had been found. Soon the authorities consulted with the fire service and were told that firefighting planes, or "water bombers," had been sent over the same stretch of water on that day. These vehicles skim the surface of the sea and collect thousands of gallons of water in huge buckets slung from the fuselage. The police realized with horror what had happened: somehow one of the water bombers had sucked the diver up into its water bucket and then dumped him into the forest fire. As he was wearing his oxygen tank, it's possible that he was still alive until he hit the ground.

AN EXTRA MEMBER OF STAFF

Staff at a London law firm had been bothered by flies in their office for days. They opened windows to let the insects out, but they seemed to be coming from somewhere inside the building. Then they started to notice a strange smell, even though the office was cleaned from top to bottom every morning. They thought that an animal might have crawled in somewhere and died, so they hired pest controllers to search for a possible rat or unfortunate stray cat. By that point the smell was so bad that an entire floor had to be left unused.

The pest controllers spotted the fireplace: it hadn't been used since the building was converted into an office many years previously, and the chimney had been blocked up to stop draughts. Maybe something had crawled into the empty space? They started to knock bricks out of the wall and when flies burst out of the hole and they were overpowered by a terrible smell, they knew they had found the source of the problem. They were horrified to discover that there was a dead body jammed in the chimney, in the early stages of decomposition. How he had got there was a mystery, but the coroner concluded that he had been in that space for several weeks.

The police had been called to the building weeks earlier to check out what they thought was a failed break-in attempt after builders reported a hole in the roof, which they suspected had been made by thieves looking to steal valuable lead cladding. It turned out that the break-in had been more successful than they had realized, and the intruder had never left the building. It was not known how he came to be inside the chimney, but at some point he had fallen and become stuck upside down in the narrow opening. He had probably suffocated before he starved.

THE SANTA TRAP

A man in California lit the fire in his hearth for the first time that winter one evening. He noticed that something was wrong when he saw smoke filling the room and assumed that something was blocking the chimney, even though it had been swept only weeks earlier. Then he heard a scrabbling noise coming from the wall and desperate cries for help. To his horror, he realized that someone was stuck up there. He frantically tried to put out the fire, eventually swamping it with a bucket of water and causing smoke to billow up while the person was still frantically trying to escape. When firefighters arrived, they tried to pull the intruder out from below, but he was too high up, so they smashed through the bricks underneath him and pulled him out. However, they were too late: he had died of smoke inhalation. Police suspected that he was a burglar who had been attempting to enter the property during the night when he thought the owner would be asleep.

LA PASCUALITA

In 1930 the owner of a shop selling bridal dresses in Chihuahua, Mexico, suffered a terrible tragedy. Her daughter was at the wedding shop on the day she was due to get married, preparing to don the intricate and beautiful dress that her mother had made for her. It was brought out of the back room and laid out carefully for the bride. She put it on, but as it was being fastened, she let out a cry of pain, holding her neck, and slumped to the floor. She never regained consciousness. An employee claimed to have seen a black widow jump from the dress after the incident and the doctor said that the girl had indeed suffered a fatal spider bite that poisoned her blood. This is only the beginning of her story, however.

Her mother was distraught and could not bear to part with her daughter so, in secret, she hatched a plan to keep her close forever. According to legend, she enlisted a local funeral parlor to deploy all their skills in embalming the girl so that she looked almost alive and then, instead of taking the body to church, she installed it in the wedding shop storeroom, where she could look at her all day.

Exactly one year after her death, which would have been the girl's first wedding anniversary, locals were greeted by a new mannequin in the dress shop. It was wearing the very same dress that the owner's daughter had been wearing when she was killed. When people who had known the girl commented on how the doll looked just like her, the owner claimed that any resemblance to her daughter was just a sad coincidence, but that she couldn't bear to get rid of that dress.

The mannequin started to attract visitors, who were drawn by her beautifully lifelike features, and soon people began to go to the shop just to gaze in wonder at La Pascualita, as she became known. Rumors began circulating that the dummy did not just look like the dead girl: it *was* the dead girl.

It was said that her eyes followed visitors around the shop as they browsed, that she would change her poses when no one was looking and that she appeared in different places each morning, as if she had been moving around when the shop was closed. One story described how a magician had fallen in love with La Pascualita and would take her out dancing at night.

The owner continued to deny it—who would do such a thing? But people who worked in the store were in no doubt that La Pascualita was more than a lifeless mannequin. When they got up close to change her dress, they would break out in a cold sweat, disturbed by her long delicate eyelashes, slightly wrinkled hands, green eyes that appeared to be wet with tears and even varicose veins on her legs. Even sceptical observers, determined to prove to others that the figure was only a mannequin, were said to be so captivated by her beauty that they left the shop convinced that she was real. After the owner died, the legend of La Pascualita continued to live on, and today people still travel from miles around to marvel at her beauty and the green eyes that follow you around the room.

QUIET IN THE LIBRARY

Jackie was a student at Penn State University. One evening she told friends that she was going to the library to revise for an exam she was due to sit. The place was busy, as it was getting close to the end of term and everybody had deadlines to meet. Jackie was a popular girl on campus and several witnesses who reported seeing her in the library that night remarked that she was her usual friendly self. Most of the students were keeping quiet, as required by the rules of the place, and had their heads stuck in their books, so nobody heard or saw anything unusual. Then a man leaving the library told the desk staff that there was somebody needing medical help on the first floor. They found Jackie lying behind a bookshelf, struggling to breathe. An ambulance was called but she died upon arrival at hospital. She had been stabbed with a narrow instrument through the heart—her red dress had concealed the bloodstains. She was attacked only a few feet from a study group, whose members claimed not to have heard or seen anything. The man who alerted the staff was never identified, even after thousands of police interviews, and the murderer has never been found.

UNDERPANTS ARE DANGEROUS

Next time you try to "pull a wedgie" on one of your friends, and yank their underpants out of their trousers, be aware that people have died in similar stunts. An American man fought with his stepfather and gave him what he called "an atomic wedgie"— when you pull the victim's underpants up over their head— causing the older man's death when the elastic from his pants became stuck around his neck and eventually suffocated him. The prankster was sent to jail for 30 years after being convicted of manslaughter.

FUNERAL FRIGHT

A Brazilian mother was mourning the untimely death of her son—a window cleaner in his thirties who, prior to his death, had not been seen for months—at a ceremony in her home in a town near São Paulo, when a surprise visitor made an entrance. Everybody present saw that he bore a striking resemblance to the man in the coffin, which caused some to faint and others to flee in horror—were they seeing a ghost?

The previous day the man's brother had read that a window cleaner had been killed in the area and, fearing it could be his brother, visited the mortuary to find out for sure. He sadly identified the dead man as his missing sibling and the rest of the family, who probably had other things on their mind, did not notice anything out of place. After all, who knows what death might do to someone's appearance? On the day of the ceremony, the window cleaner—alive and well, and back in town—bumped into a friend in the street, who told him in disbelief that he was about to miss his own funeral. He telephoned another acquaintance, who happened to be at the ceremony, but the call was dismissed as a cruel hoax. Back from the dead, the man decided to put things to rest, so to speak, and turned up at his mother's house in person, becoming the guest of honor at his own funeral. The identity of the poor man in the coffin was never determined.

CAUTIONARY TALES

STRANGER DANGER

Two Scottish men travelling on business in Texas were celebrating the end of their trip with a night out on the town. When the bar closed, they decided to continue the party, so they flagged down a taxi to take them back to their hotel, but they soon became paranoid, thinking that they were being driven in the wrong direction. So they asked the driver to stop and headed out into the night on their own, finding themselves completely lost in a quiet residential neighborhood. This was before mobile phones were commonplace, so the businessmen began knocking on doors to see if they could use someone's phone to call another taxi. Having no success, they ventured into a back garden to get someone's attention. Back home in Scotland they were used to leaving their doors unlocked, so this didn't strike them as particularly unsafe—and certainly not after drinking all night. The homeowner, woken by the noise, came downstairs and saw two men peering in through his back door at 4 a.m., and he didn't think twice about firing his shotgun, killing them outright.

A SHOCKING TALE

A young extreme sports enthusiast, who was covered in a variety of piercings, tattoos and body modifications, was always looking for the next adrenaline rush. One day while he was at work on a construction site, he bet his colleagues that he would clip two electrical lines to his piercings and give himself a thrill. They tried to persuade him that it wasn't a good idea, but this only made him more determined. Unaware that by applying electricity directly to his chest he was at risk of experiencing more than just a funny sensation, he attached the electrical lines to each of his pierced nipples and promptly received a fatal shock through the heart from which he could not be revived.

LAWN CHAIR LIFT-OFF

Sometimes life really is like the movies. In 1982 a man from Los Angeles had a moment of inspiration that almost cost him his life. He had been chewing the fat with friends at a bar, speculating about how many balloons it would take to lift a man into the sky. As flying happened to be a long-held dream of his, he decided to purchase 40 balloons of the type that scientists launch into the clouds to research the weather and give it a try—after all, apart from his life, he had nothing to lose.

So he went ahead with his plan and attached the bunch of balloons to his favorite lawn chair, ballasted with plastic water bottles. He estimated that he would be able to hover a couple of storeys off the ground and carried an air pistol on board to burst the balloons, should the altitude become unnerving. He settled into his chair while he plucked up the courage to tell his friends to let go of the lines keeping him on the ground, but all of a sudden, the ropes snapped and the balloons were caught by a gust of wind. Before he could do anything about it, the lawn chair had surged to an altitude of 16,000 feet, while its pilot clung on for dear life. He called for help on a radio and began shooting the balloons, but then he dropped the pistol, leaving him at the mercy of the wind. After dodging some surprised birds and being spotted by concerned airline pilots coming in to land at an airport, he collided with power lines, causing a minor blackout, and eventually landed 15 miles away from where he had taken off. He had spent more than an hour in the sky and, apart from being a little shocked, he had escaped unharmed. The adventure of a lifetime was over and he had an unlikely tale to tell his friends—but he did face a fine from the aviation authorities over his unauthorised trip, once they decided which law he had broken.

ALWAYS READ THE LABEL

You should always make sure that a job is done properly. A barman tasked with cleaning the toilets in an old British pub was not keen on the job so looked for ways to cut a few corners—an approach that almost cost him his life. He had a brainwave, and mixed bleach and descaling solution together in order to kill two birds with one stone. However, he almost killed himself as well in the process. When he poured the concoction into the toilets, he was concerned to see an evil-looking vapor rising out of the cubicles that made his eyes sting and his lungs burn, so he made a swift exit. He barely made it out of the bathroom before evacuating the pub and passing out. Firefighters who attended the scene explained that in his effort to speed up the job, he had unwittingly created chlorine gas—the lethal vapor used in the trenches of World War One—and he was lucky to have escaped with his life.

BOOK BINDING

An 1852 collection of poems by John Milton, the author of *Paradise Lost*, which can be found in Devon, England, looks like any other old book, but it is unique for a disturbing reason: it's bound in leather made from the skin of a convicted murderer. In 1830 George Cudmore was found guilty of murdering his wife. The rat catcher, a reportedly short and hunchbacked individual, had used poison to do away with his spouse so that he could be with his lover. George was sentenced to be hanged and also told that his body would be taken to a local hospital, where it would be used for experiments. It's not entirely clear how Cudmore ended up as a book cover 20 years later. The volume, containing many religious works, bears an inscription that tells readers whose skin they are holding, perhaps as a warning to keep them on the straight and narrow.

GUILTY AS CHARGED

Have you ever put a nine-volt battery to your tongue to feel the tiny electric shock it gives you? If so, next time you should probably think twice: that little battery could kill you. A US Navy sailor was in an electronics class when he picked up two prongs attached to a nine-volt battery, intending to demonstrate the electrical resistance of the human body. Pressing each probe with his thumbs, he made a fatal mistake: he gripped so tightly that the pointed probes pierced his skin, and he got a terrible shock. He learned the hard way that the skin provides most of the body's resistance to electricity, as your insides, being largely made of water, conduct electricity quite well. Bypassing the skin allowed the charge to go straight into his bloodstream and a fatal shock crossed his heart, killing him instantly. His story is retold to all new recruits, warning them not to fool around with equipment.

DON'T DRINK THE WATER

When you are abroad in a strange country, in a strange hotel, you expect things to be a little different to life back home. "Don't drink the tap water" is something that you will commonly be told. But you probably wouldn't expect to hear that in Los Angeles. In 2013 tourists at a hotel in LA had noticed that something was a little odd: the pressure was weak and the water in the shower would run black for a while before turning clear. It also had a funny taste and smelled unusual. Nevertheless, they drank it, as they assumed that was just how water in LA was supposed to taste.

Eventually, someone complained to staff at the hotel, who sent a worker to check whether the four large water tanks on the roof were in good order. What he found when he opened the lid turned his stomach, but it certainly explained the issues they had been having: inside one of the cisterns was a partially decomposed human body. The unfortunate maintenance man had found the remains of a female student who had gone missing after staying in the hotel several weeks previously. Guests at the establishment had been using corpse-water to shower and brush their teeth for weeks, as well as drinking it. Pathologists determined that the student had drowned in the water, so she wasn't killed before ending up in the heavy-lidded tank. But how had she ended up there? Investigators were baffled. They had the girl on camera on the night she was last seen by other guests, and she appeared agitated. She was pictured in an elevator, and peeking into the corridor, as if she didn't want to be seen, but then pressing all the buttons. It shouldn't have been possible for her to even get on the roof, as it was a locked and restricted area. As there were no more leads, her death remains a mystery to this day.

CRUISE CONTROL

A young couple from France were honeymooning in the United States. It was their dream to hire a big American motor home and go on a road trip across the country. They found the perfect vehicle, and after the salesman had shown them the two showers, cable TV, king-size bed and cruise control, they wasted no time in getting on the road. A few days later they were travelling across the desert overnight, and the husband had gone to sleep for a few hours while his new wife took the wheel.

It wasn't long before the long empty roads and the warmth of the night made her feel sleepy, so she decided to make a coffee. She didn't want to wake her partner so she found the cruise control button, flicked it on and went to make the drink. She never made it back to her seat. The vehicle left the road at the next corner and was found a week later in a mangled heap at the bottom of a rocky ravine. The girl didn't know that the cruise control couldn't handle corners, and the truck had simply plunged over the precipice. Neither honeymooner survived.

WAKE UP AND SMELL THE PERFUME

A warning circulated online, advising American women to be wary of strangers when visiting shopping malls. It followed news reports of a number of middle-aged ladies being approached by smartly dressed men in the car parks of malls who asked them for advice on a perfume that they were thinking of buying for their wives or girlfriends. It turned out that the small perfume bottles or handkerchiefs that the men were carrying weren't filled with the latest fashionable eau de toilette, but with an intense mixture of chloroform. When the ladies smelled the scent, they became instantly incapacitated. Some were abducted, bundled into the back of a van, driven to remote locations and tortured for their bank details, whereas others were robbed and left for dead in the car park. The report quoted a police source saying that even men who had a female partner with them could not be trusted, as the women were likely in on the scam.

DON'T TRY THIS AT HOME

You may know the trick of making a bottle of cola explode by dropping a packet of mints into it and screwing the cap back on, but you may not know how dangerous it can be. When the internet recently sparked a new cola-mint craze, kids in playgrounds around the world started creating bigger and bigger explosions to post online. In one school in England, this led to tragic consequences.

The young boy involved, referred to as Billy in the papers, was known as the joker of the class and renowned at his school for doing absolutely anything that fellow pupils dared him to. They decided to use him as a guinea pig to see what happened when you combined cola and mints not in a bottle, but in the human body. The ingredients were prepared—a 2-liter bottle of drink and a big bag of mints—and a large crowd gathered in the playground. Billy ate the entire bag of sweets first and washed that down with as much cola as he could manage.

At first everything seemed fine, and the assembled kids cheered, but then Billy groaned and bent over with terrible cramps, rolling around on the floor. Witnesses reported that his eyes appeared to bulge out of his head. He tried to bring up the noxious liquid but it was too late. He gave a final sharp cry of pain and died on the spot. Investigators were able to explain the cause of the tragedy: when you add mints to cola, the ingredients in the sweets break the surface tension of the liquid, which is what prevents the pressurised carbon dioxide—which creates the bubbles—from escaping all at once. The mints therefore cause a sudden and violent release of gas, which is what makes the liquid explode out of the bottles. By ingesting the cola and mints together in such large quantities, Billy had caused a huge build-up of gas in his abdomen, far too large to escape through the usual channels, and his stomach had exploded in seconds. It was advised that nobody try to recreate the stunt at home.

A SARTORIAL SURPRISE

Staff at a chain of clothes stores in Australia were inundated with hundreds of calls from concerned customers after an incident at one of their shops. A woman had been trying on a jacket for winter, when she felt a sharp prick in her arm. She assumed it was a stray pin and complained to the assistant, who apologised and said she would look into it. The customer thought nothing of it, but on her drive home her heart rate suddenly dropped, she blacked out and crashed the car. She was in a coma for a month. The doctors were confused at first, as she had no visible injuries from the crash, but her blood results indicated that she showed all the signs of having venom in her system.

It was not a pin in the jacket: it was a poisonous snake that had bitten her as she tried the garment on. The store was shut and police found an adder in the arm of the jacket, which had been put back on the rack so that another customer could have put it on. The deadly snake had found its way into the lining of the jacket when it was looking for somewhere to hibernate, and it was very hungry.

ELECTRIC BLANKETS

A warning was put out on social media, claiming that a certain brand of electric blanket was being recalled across Europe after a safety scare. A mother who had recently bought the item to keep her toddler warm was woken by his screams one night. She rushed into his room and found him clinging to the bars of his cot, trying to escape from a small hissing snake. The reptile was an exotic tiger snake, highly venomous, and not native to the country. An investigation discovered that the blanket, which had been manufactured in Asia, had become infested with snake eggs that were not easily detectable from the outside. Cold conditions on the ship that transported the products to Europe had kept the animals in a state of hibernation, but when the blanket was turned on, the pleasant warmth encouraged the eggs to hatch, and the baby snakes were soon looking for their first meal.

THE ENVELOPE

A woman had a job in a New York post office, where she spent all day attending to customers and licking an awful lot of stamps. One day she lost concentration and cut her tongue on an envelope. Later that day, returning home after work, she realized that her tongue had become swollen, and she found it difficult to eat. Visits to the doctor did not reveal the source of the problem, but eventually she reached the point when she could not even drink so she made an emergency visit to the local hospital. The medics were perplexed and took an X-ray of her mouth. They rushed back to her and told her that she needed emergency surgery or she may soon lose the ability to breathe as well. They put the woman under anesthetic and when they sliced into the swelling, hundreds of tiny baby spiders crawled out onto her face. The doctors had to suck them out of her throat with a vacuum pump. It transpired that the envelope came from a batch which had been kept in a South American warehouse, where the paper had been contaminated by eggs from a highly poisonous wolf spider. When the woman licked the paper seal, the eggs transferred to her mouth in her saliva, and the cut on her tongue became the perfect place for them to grow. They would soon have hatched of their own accord. All of the envelopes from that warehouse were recalled before somebody else suffered the same fate.

WATCH OUT FOR CRUMBS

Doctors in Taiwan warned of the dangers of eating food in bed, after two cases ended up in local hospitals. A man, who was admitted to a ward for a routine foot operation, was addicted to snacks, and was repeatedly told by the nurses not to hide food and empty packets in his bedclothes, because they could attract ants. He ignored them—he wasn't scared of ants—but soon after his operation he found himself back in hospital, complaining of terrible headaches that no amount of drugs could treat. When doctors scanned his brain for abnormalities, they were horrified to discover a mass of black insects inside his ear canals. A colony of ants, attracted by his snacks, had entered his ears when he was recuperating from his operation and were gradually eating away at the insides of his skull; he would have lost his hearing had doctors not located the infestation in time.

The authorities highlighted another similar report: a 14-year-old girl complained of severe earache, and her mother explained that she had a sweet tooth and often ate midnight snacks in bed, despite being told not to. Upon inspection, the doctor found thousands of ants packed deep in her ear: they had crawled there in search of food and died.

DANGEROUS DEPOSITS

Canadian citizens received email warnings after a woman reportedly died after licking an envelope when making a deposit in a Toronto bank. The message quoted a police officer who said that investigators had found traces of rat poison in the dead woman's system and, by retracing her steps that day, they had narrowed the source down to the glue she had licked while making a deposit at the bank. As a result, the establishment was closed and all envelopes were seized. However, a rumor then spread that this wasn't an isolated incident so a number of banks announced that, while they had no evidence of any envelopes being tampered with, they had since switched to ones that didn't need licking.

I THINK THIS IS YOURS

Police in New York publicised a tale they had heard from a member of the public in order to warn others. A young man visited a 24-hour convenience store late one night on his way home from the city. He found a parking spot some distance away and walked to the shop, checking his wallet as he went. The store was empty—even the assistant was not there—save for one other man: an older gentleman with grey hair, who appeared to be aimlessly browsing the shelves, as he had nothing in his basket.

The young man made his selections, paid at the automatic checkout and then set off down the road towards his car; he reported later that he felt as though he was being watched. He was just about to start the engine when there was a knock on the window. It was the old man from the store, holding a $20 bill. The driver rolled the window down a little and the man smiled. "I think you dropped this," he said, waving the money around.

"I don't think so. I always know how much money I'm carrying. Thanks, though," replied the young man politely and wound the window back up. He had checked his wallet before he went in the shop and he didn't have a $20 bill in there. As he started the car, the man knocked on the window again and repeated, "I think you dropped this." Although the driver wanted to pull away, the road was busy and as he waited, the man knocked on the window again, still repeating, "I think you dropped this."

Why was the old man doing that? Why was he so insistent?

While waiting for a gap in the traffic, the driver opened the window to tell the man to keep the money, because it wasn't his, but he noticed that he was no longer greeted by a smile but by a scowl. As the older gentleman started to tug at the top of the open window, trying to thrust a hand inside and open the door, the driver hurried to close it, so the strange man began to bang his elbow on it. The young man thought that the glass was going to break, so he put his foot on the accelerator, almost causing an accident as he joined the busy road.

At first the youngster didn't tell anybody about the incident; he wasn't entirely sure what had happened anyway. Eventually, he decided to go to the police station and make a report. When the authorities heard his story, they agreed that the older man's behavior was bizarre and checked the CCTV recording from the shop, only to find it had been wiped. There was nothing more they could do apart from warning the public. Besides, they doubted whether a crime had actually been committed—and was he sure that the money wasn't his after all?

Several days later a retired detective rang the station after reading the report in the paper. He said that it probably didn't mean anything, but the story was ringing a bell with him. When he was in the force, he had worked on a case, long since closed, concerning the death of a young man. The victim had been abducted, murdered and dumped in his own car. The last person to see him alive witnessed him being handed money that he had apparently dropped on the street by a Good Samaritan. The police recommended that everybody be aware at all times of the money they are carrying.

GOODBYE MUM

A young woman from South London posted the following tale on social media as a warning to others. She was in a busy supermarket doing her weekly shop when she noticed an elderly lady following her around and smiling. At first the girl ignored her, thinking that perhaps the old lady was not quite all there, but as this went on for a while, the girl asked if she could help her with anything; after all, she had noticed that the lady was pushing a large trolley full of food. The elderly woman apologised for being a nuisance, but said she couldn't help noticing that the girl looked just like someone she knew.

The girl became curious and asked who it was so the lady explained that she was the spitting image of her daughter, who had died several months earlier. Now she was in full flow, telling the younger woman how she missed her child terribly, how it was all made more unbearable because she had not been able to say goodbye and how the last time she had seen her they had parted on bad terms. Unfortunately, she hadn't been able to make it to the hospital because of her own painful medical condition. The girl expressed her sympathies and got on with her shopping. She felt guilty for not doing more, but was unsure what to say.

Then the old lady started to attract the attention of the other shoppers with her crying, so the girl walked back to her and tried to comfort her, apologising if she had upset her. The lady asked if she could walk around with the girl while she did her shopping; she wouldn't be any bother, but it might make her feel a little bit better. It was the least the young lady could do, so she took her around the shop and tried to make small talk. Once they reached the till, the elderly woman went in line first. As the girl helped her unload her trolley, she was asked for one more thing: could she say, "Goodbye, Mum" as the woman left? The girl thought it an odd request but felt as if she owed her something and agreed.

As the girl packed the old lady's items back into her trolley, she saw her whisper something in the ear of the cashier before moving towards the exit. The girl called after her as promised, "Bye Mum!" The lady smiled and went on her way, and the young woman felt as if she had done her good deed for the day. She packed up her own shopping and the cashier told her the total. When she saw the amount, she assumed there had been some mistake: although there were only a few items in her basket, the bill was well over £100. The cashier explained that there had been no error; the extra cost was down to her mother's shopping. The girl asked what she meant, but it slowly began to dawn on her what had happened.

"Your mother said that you—her daughter—were picking up the bill. That's so good of you." The young woman looked towards the door but the old lady was nowhere to be seen. The cashier wouldn't let her look in the car park without settling the bill, so the girl had no choice but to pay up.

SMART THIEVES

An email circulated a few years ago, warning about how smart criminals were getting in today's digital age and telling motorists to be more vigilant than usual; car thieves are not just smashing windows these days.

A man had parked his car at a swimming pool. He worked as a security guard and followed his usual careful procedure: he parked in the far corner of the lot, where his car wouldn't bring attention to itself, shut his satnav in the glovebox after using it, where it couldn't be seen by thieves, and put his wallet in the center console, as he didn't trust the flimsy lockers at the swimming pool. The man returned to the car after his swim and didn't notice anything amiss. The next day he needed to travel to a new office for work so he needed to use his satnav again—but it was not in the glovebox. He was sure that was the last place where he had left it but, after a fruitless search everywhere, he realized that it must have been stolen. How could that have happened, though? There was no sign of anybody breaking into the car.

He eventually convinced himself that he must have left the vehicle unlocked in the swimming pool car park and accepted the loss of the device. Some days later he returned home from work to find his front door wide open and his house in disarray. There had been a break-in, and they had taken everything of any value from the downstairs rooms. The police concluded that the thieves were obviously professionals and that they must have known he wouldn't be at home. The officers asked if anything unusual had happened in the previous days, such as somebody tampering with his car, so he told them about the satnav and they suggested taking a look at his vehicle.

They went straight to the passenger-side door and beckoned him over. There was a tiny hole under the lock, barely visible unless you were looking for it, resembling a bullet hole. The officers explained how the scam worked: thieves used custom-made air guns to punch holes through the lock, opening the car door with no fuss in half a second. It only worked on certain models, but they knew exactly what they were looking for. The criminals even locked the car doors again, so as not to arouse the victim's suspicions and thus leaving plenty of time for them to carry out their plan. Indeed, once inside, they were even craftier: they located the satnav, found the car owner's home address in the system and visited at another time, breaking in when the car was not on the drive and therefore the owner was unlikely to be at home.

The thieves also had a habit of stealing credit cards—never the whole wallet and never all the cards. Had he checked his? He was certain his wallet was safe, but sure enough, one of the credit cards that he rarely used was missing. In a panic he rang the company and was told that the thieves had run up thousands of dollars' worth of charges in only a few hours on the day that the satnav went missing.

The man asked the police why they had targeted his vehicle, as he never left valuables on display, but they said that it was just bad luck. This method of entry was so quick and easy that thieves tried it on as many cars as they dared, and most people never even noticed the hole.

The email ended by warning drivers to keep a close eye on their door locks, never to leave their home address in a satnav—or at least never label it as such—and to park their cars in highly visible places where potential thieves might be noticed.

OPERA TICKETS

A successful middle-aged couple had moved to a neighborhood in the suburbs. They had recently bought a new BMW SUV and parked it prominently in front of their new abode. They were going out to a restaurant to celebrate moving into their new house, and some friends picked them up. When they returned, they were shocked to find that the car had disappeared off the drive. The police arrived but the officers didn't hold out much hope of finding it in one piece; such desirable motors were stolen by joyriders, ram-raiders or professional thieves. So imagine the pair's surprise when they opened the curtains the next morning to find the BMW parked exactly where they had left it, apparently without a scratch.

There was an envelope under the wipers. Inside was a letter from a man who said that he was sorry for taking the car without asking, but his own vehicle had broken down in the street with his pregnant wife inside. She had gone into labor without warning, so they were left with no other option but to find another car. They knocked at the door for help, and couldn't help noticing that it was open and that the BMW keys were on the hall table, so they took the vehicle to get to the hospital. The car owner was understandably suspicious until he read to the end of the note and saw what else was in the envelope. The letter ended, "Please accept these tickets as a peace offering"—inside there were two tickets to the opera, which the couple happened to love.

On the night of the performance, they got dressed to the nines and, thinking they deserved a proper celebration, got a taxi into town. When they returned, they couldn't believe their eyes: once again the BMW had disappeared. They wondered whether they had fallen victim to some bizarre scam so they went inside the house to call the police, but their night was about to get worse. The front door was open and they found an envelope in the letterbox. Inside was a simple note: "Hope you enjoyed the opera." The entire house had been ransacked.

EMERGENCY STOP

One night in 1970, a young woman was driving on a California highway with her ten-month-old daughter beside her. They were visiting the woman's mother in the next town and, as it was late, there were few cars on the road. The saloon behind her had been following for a few miles. Suddenly, the driver began flashing his lights and repeatedly sounding the horn. The young mother, assuming that he was just an impatient driver, pulled over and slowed to let him pass, but he stayed behind, still honking his horn. She reluctantly stopped and the other car pulled up behind her. The driver stepped out of his vehicle and walked up to her window, which she lowered a couple of inches. He was a man— about 30-years-old, with spectacles and rather ordinary-looking— and he told her that he had been trying to get her to stop because her rear wheel was wobbling. It looked like the nuts were loose and it would be dangerous to continue.

The man offered to sort out the problem for her, as it wouldn't take long and the woman wouldn't even have to get out of the car. She agreed; she hadn't noticed anything wrong with the way the car was driving, but she didn't want to take any risks with her daughter in the vehicle. The man went to his boot, retrieved a wrench and got to work. Once he had finished, he waved her onto the highway again and soon she couldn't see his car in her mirrors, but all of a sudden, she heard an almighty knocking noise and the car started to judder badly. Her daughter started crying and she veered onto the hard shoulder, skidding to a halt. She could see in her mirrors that one of the wheels had fallen off.

She was wondering what to do next when a car pulled over in front of her: it was the man who had supposedly fixed her wheel. He apologised, saying that it must have been worse than he thought—he wasn't a professional mechanic, after all— and offered to drive her to the nearest garage to get help. She decided that she didn't have many other options and climbed into his car with her daughter. They soon passed a garage, but the man missed the turn-off, and then they passed a couple more. When the woman asked why he wasn't stopping, he changed the subject. This went on for some time, and the woman began to panic. Finally, he stopped at a junction, so she had enough time to grab her daughter and flee the car, running into a nearby cornfield. She could hear him calling for her, and saw the light from his torch, but the crops were high enough to hide her presence. Eventually, he got back into his car and drove off. After making sure that he was not coming back, the young mother flagged down another motorist and asked to be taken to the nearest police station, where she recounted the evening's events to the officer on duty.

The policeman explained that there had probably been nothing wrong with her car until the man stopped her and loosened all the nuts on the wheel—afterwards, all he had to do was wait for it to fall off. As the officer was talking, the woman noticed a wanted poster on the station noticeboard. The face on it looked identical to the man on the highway. He was the suspect in a brutal murder, who would later become famous as the Zodiac Killer: the unknown serial killer who sent cryptic notes to the *San Francisco Chronicle* about his crimes. A few months later the paper received one referring to the "woman and her baby that I gave a rather interesting ride for a couple of hours one evening." The woman's car was located again; it was burned out. The Zodiac Killer was never identified and may still be at large.

MIND THE GAP

A young professional was taking the last train home on the London Underground one night. The carriage was almost empty for once, but at the next stop three people boarded, who appeared to be high or drunk and were stumbling around. They sat directly opposite the woman and she avoided eye contact, as she didn't want a scene. The train pulled away from the platform and after a while she began to feel that someone was watching her. She saw out of the corner of her eye that the woman sitting across from her was staring blankly in her direction. This made her feel uncomfortable, but she pretended not to notice and didn't react. Nevertheless, every time she looked, the woman was still staring. She wanted to get off but that was the last train, and moving seats wasn't a solution either, as it might have attracted unwanted attention.

Then a man came down the carriage and sat next to her. He leaned in and quietly told her that she should get off at the next station. She asked him why, and he told her to trust him, because something wasn't quite right with the train. The next stop was at a busy intersection so she agreed. As soon as they were off the train, the man apologised if he had scared her, but he had had no choice: the woman sitting opposite her wasn't staring, he explained: she was dead. She was propped up between the two men. He had seen them get on the train, and she had a terrible wound in the back of her head. The girl later found out that the two men had been arrested for the woman's murder, who hadn't been their first victim that night.

RAZOR BLADES

A water park in Germany, with a large pool and many flumes, was closed down after its main attraction, the "black hole," down which kids used to slide in complete darkness, caused several nasty injuries to members of the public. Razor blades were found embedded in its side, which were slicing swimmers as they slid past. Many didn't realise that they had been cut until they saw the plunge pool at the bottom of the slide turn red with blood. Similar incidents have been widely reported in America and England.

BABY-TRIPPER

The replacement babysitter had arrived. She was late, but she was all they could get at short notice. The girl had come recommended by one of Jennifer's friends at work, who said that although she might come across as a little ditsy, and was a bit of a "hippy," she was great with children. Her appearance didn't quite match what they were used to from their usual prim-and-proper sitters—she had face piercings and dreadlocks—but they were late for dinner so they were left with no choice. They could always call in a while to make sure that everything was OK. Jennifer told her that there was chicken in the fridge if she was hungry.

Later on in the evening Pete called home to check on the girl, but she said that everything was groovy and that she'd even put the chicken in the oven for them. He thought that was a bit odd, but didn't dwell on the conversation any further and went back inside the restaurant. When they got home, they were appalled to find the babysitter lying on the carpet in the living room, staring blankly into space and murmuring. She was clearly high on something and couldn't be woken from her reverie. They ran upstairs to check on the baby, but she was nowhere to be found. They started to panic, shaking the sitter to get her to talk, but she was not responding. Then Pete noticed that the oven light was on. It was the only place where they hadn't looked. He wrenched the door open and to his horror saw the baby inside, wrapped in foil. Luckily, the babysitter had been so away with the fairies that she hadn't turned on the gas.

A FEAR OF CONFINED SPACES

A team of maintenance workers in Xi'an, China, had been working on a building site for a few weeks and they needed to examine the lift shafts. As they entered, they were taken aback by a terrible odor. One of them remarked that it smelled like something had died in there, and as they explored further, that's exactly what they found. They tracked the smell to a lift stuck halfway between two floors, and were expecting to find an animal that had found its way into the empty building and become trapped. With difficulty, they prised open the door and had to cover their faces as the powerful stench hit them. They were shocked to see a woman's corpse slumped in the corner of the lift. With rising horror, they gradually realized what had happened to her.

They had first arrived at the site a month earlier and, before starting work, they were supposed to check whether anyone was still in the lift. Evidently, they had failed to do so, so when they cut off the power, the woman had become trapped. As she lived alone, nobody reported her missing; the building was empty of its usual workers, so nobody could hear her cries, and the emergency alarm system was rendered useless by the power cut. It's not known how long the woman had survived alone in the lift before her death. The guilty workers were convicted of corporate manslaughter.

THE SHOPPING MALL MAN

A warning was circulated on the internet, issued by a woman who reported an unsettling experience at her local giant shopping mall. She had visited on a Saturday to do her regular shop and on returning to her car, she was upset to find that she had a flat tyre, especially as it was relatively new. She opened the boot of her car, retrieved the spare tyre and the wheel wrench, and set to work.

However, as the garage had fitted the wheel using an air gun to tighten the nuts, she was having trouble loosening them and couldn't budge them at all. She was about to give up and call for help when a smartly dressed man carrying a briefcase appeared and asked if she needed a hand. She explained the situation and he said that he would have a go, suggesting that she should wait in the car, but she wanted to watch how he did it. He was heavily built and managed to remove the tyre in no time, chatting to her about how mechanics always fastened the nuts too tightly. She took up his offer of attaching the spare as well, and he put the flat tyre in her boot and closed it.

The woman thanked him and was ready to set off on her way, when she noticed that the man no longer had his briefcase. She assumed that he must have dropped it in her boot. When she reminded him, he said that his own car was actually parked all the way on the other side of the car park, and he asked if she wouldn't mind giving him a quick lift round. Then he would get the case. She thought it was a slightly odd request, but she was so grateful for his help that it would have been churlish to decline. He told her that he was only in that part of the mall because he had got lost when looking for the food court and had ended up walking out of the wrong exit.

They both got in her car and she drove slowly through the car park. The woman claimed to be paranoid about the spare wheel falling off and insisted that she wanted to get out to check that the nuts were still tight. The man assured her they'd be fine, but she stopped the car outside the main entrance and got out. She took a cursory glance at the wheel before running back into the mall as fast as she could, taking the car keys with her. She made straight for the guard's office and explained that there was a strange man in her car who was making her uncomfortable. He had changed her tyre, but he was giving her far too many details, which made her suspicious, and he had locked his briefcase in her boot, she believed on purpose.

The guard strode out to her car and, sure enough, the man had disappeared without his case, which they took back to the office to examine. The woman gasped as she saw the contents: a rope, a sharp knife and some kind of bottled chemical.

It had all been a front to get inside her car. She wondered what would have happened if she had done as he had asked and stayed in the car, where she wouldn't have noticed him dropping his briefcase in her boot. Later she learned that the air had been let out of the tyre deliberately; there was no puncture. What the man had planned for her was a sinister mystery, but the authorities deemed it a sufficiently serious case to warn the wider public. He had failed that time, but was sure to try again.

THE LONG ARM OF THE LAW

I REST MY CASE

A hotshot lawyer with a long career in politics is remembered chiefly for the last and most important case he ever took on. He was defending a disreputable character accused of bursting into an illegal card game at a local bar and shooting dead one of the players, who happened to be one of his old enemies. It was widely regarded as an open-and-shut case, but the lawyer refused to be beaten and went to the trouble of conducting his own ballistics experiments—using his pistol—to prove that his client could not have been the killer. He had examined the dead man's gun and was certain that he had in fact shot himself in the stomach when trying to draw it from his pocket. When the moment came for him to declare his theory in court, he assumed the same pose as the victim, placed a gun in his pocket, drew, pulled the trigger and shot himself in the stomach. "My God, I've shot myself," he cried in pain.

He had obviously thought that the gun was unloaded, but he had mixed it up with another one that morning. His dedicated demonstration won him the case: the accused was acquitted, but the lawyer died the next day from his wounds.

TOUGH COOKIE

A British lawyer was celebrating winning another case at an expensive Chinese restaurant in London with his colleagues. At the end of the meal he opened the customary fortune cookie and scoffed at the contents, which read, "Your greatest asset is your sense of humor." The solicitor disagreed and was highly offended that the cookie did not tell his fortune as promised. Displaying that good sense of humor, he began legal proceedings against the restaurant and received his fortune in the end, in the form of £10,000 in damages for false advertising. In a statement, the Chinese restaurant admitted that the fortune cookie had been wrong, as the customer clearly had no sense of humor.

BAD DRIVER

Police in Ireland issued a warrant for the arrest of a Polish man, described as one of the worst serial driving offenders in the history of the country. He had been stopped for more than 50 offences in only a couple of years, right across the country, including speeding, dangerous driving and parking violations. Somehow he had evaded the clutches of the law by giving a different address each time. A few days after the news had spread, an anonymous Polish man called the hotline to explain that the name they were looking for, a Mr Prawo Jazdy, actually meant "driving licence" in Polish; in fact Mr Jazdy didn't exist. Every time a Polish person was stopped by police and handed over their licence, cops had read "Prawo Jazdy" and mistakenly assumed it to be the driver's name.

THE UNITED STATES vs SATAN

In the 1970s, an American man filed a lawsuit against "Satan and his servants" in a Pennsylvania court, asserting: "Satan has on numerous occasions caused plaintiff misery [...] placed deliberate obstacles in his path and has caused plaintiff's downfall." Surprisingly, the court decided that the verdict was "Prayer denied," and the case was dismissed. The judge explained, "The court has serious doubts that the complaint reveals a cause of action upon which relief can be granted." He questioned whether the court could actually obtain jurisdiction over the Devil, and the plaintiff had not included instructions on how Satan could be served with court papers. In the judgement he referred to a previous case in which Satan was named as defendant, where it was claimed that he was a "foreign prince with no standing to sue in an American Court"—a reference to the short story *The Devil and Daniel Webster* about a farmer who sells his soul to Lucifer.

ANIMALS ON TRIAL

In 2016 it was reported that a vulture had been arrested in Lebanon on suspicion of spying for Israel. The unfortunate bird was later freed after it was deemed not to pose a threat, but it wasn't the first animal in the region to be detained as a security threat. Another vulture and even a dolphin had been accused of the same crime over the years.

Putting animals in the dock for human crimes is a phenomenon that has been seen throughout history.

▶ In 2008 a donkey was jailed in Mexico after kicking two men. It was not freed from custody until its owner agreed to compensate the victims for any medical charges incurred in the attack.

▶ In early twentieth-century Switzerland, a dog was charged with murder, alongside two human accomplices. Rather unfairly, the animal was sentenced to death, while the humans got away with life imprisonment.

▶ In sixteenth-century France a female pig was put on trial dressed in human clothes, charged, along with her piglets, with the death of a human child. The sow was executed by hanging from a tree, but her young were spared.

▶ In 1452 the French town of Rouvre suspected a goat of being the "ringleader" of a group of cows that caused "much mischief" in the locality. The unfortunate mammal was sentenced to death.

▶ In fifteenth-century Switzerland, a rooster was found guilty of the "heinous and unnatural crime of laying an egg." The public thought it might be the spawn of Satan, and the cockerel was burnt at the stake, presumably in time for lunch.

▶ In 1519, a group of moles were put on trial in Italy after being suspected of damaging a farmer's field. Thankfully, they had a lawyer and were exiled after escaping death row.

▶ In the same decade, the French town of Autun charged all rats in the locality with the crime of damaging crops. The rodents got lucky because the lawyer assigned to their case, an ambitious politician, decided to make a name for himself and successfully argued that the rats couldn't be expected to turn up at the courthouse, as the threat of attack from the town's cats was too high. Unsurprisingly, the case was thrown out.

▶ In nineteenth-century Croatia, a captured locust was charged with the damage caused by its swarm and condemned to death by drowning.

However, it's not all doom and gloom for animal defendants. In 1750 a female donkey was charged with bestiality after a Frenchman had "relations" with the animal. The man was found guilty and sentenced to death by hanging. In normal circumstances the donkey would also have been executed, but as locals attested to the honest nature of the animal, she was spared.

FACIAL HAIR IS NO JOKE

A Russian man found fame when he copyrighted a particular type of beard. He claimed rights over the style covering the chin and the upper lip, with no sideburns, more commonly known in the West as a "goatee." He regarded it as a uniquely Russian fashion that should only be worn proudly by his countrymen. He demanded that if foreigners wore the beard, they would have to pay him a fee. Moreover, he requested that television stations obtain a licence to merely feature people wearing goatees and also that the books of famous author Paulo Coelho—a well-known goatee wearer—be removed from bookshelves in Russia unless the writer paid a "beard royalty."

CARD SHARK

An American man who was convicted of embezzling half a million dollars from his customers was due to be jailed. He tried to delay the inevitable by claiming that he was a top poker player and therefore should be allowed to try to repay his victims with the winnings from poker tournaments. Obviously his luck was in, as incredibly the judge agreed, allowing him to travel to tournaments across the country to see how his good fortune would hold up. If successful, his sentence would be reduced. If he failed to win anything, he would go straight to jail. After six months of games, he admitted that he hadn't won a single penny, so he was finally jailed for the full ten-year sentence.

THE GOVERNMENT

DOUGHNUT DIPLOMACY

It's said that the then President of the United States John F. Kennedy made a visit to Berlin, Germany, at the height of the Cold War and gave a speech in which he wished to express his solidarity with the people of the city, which was at that time split between West and East by the infamous wall. He told the assembled crowd that he felt like an honorary citizen of the city, or "Ich bin ein Berliner." The story goes that a Berliner was a popular type of German pastry, much like a doughnut, and that his heartfelt speech was greeted with nervous laughter. The President's supposed gaffe became famous around the world, but in fact he had used the correct language: although a Berliner is a German pastry, that is not the name generally used in Berlin.

CASTRO'S CIGARS

Fidel Castro, born in 1926, survived more than 600 ingenious attempts on his life carried out by Cuba's enemies, usually the

CIA. The most famous method of attempted assassination was smuggling explosives inside his favored Cuban cigars, which he gave up smoking in 1985 out of concern for his health. Another idea was to inject his cigars with a lethal botulinum toxin.

Alongside the usual plans of shooting and planting bombs at public appearances, other more creative ideas were often entertained. Scuba-diving was another of Castro's passions, so they tried to plant exploding rocks at his favorite diving sites. Plots on a similar theme involved explosives disguised as colorful mussels that they hoped he would collect, supplying a wetsuit contaminated with a toxic fungus to poison him when he put it on and infecting his breathing apparatus with a deadly disease. On learning that he chewed the end of his fountain pen, they attempted to poison that too, as well as his favorite ice-cream flavor. An attempt involving a poisonous milkshake failed after the deadly drink was put in the freezer rather than the fridge, rendering it undrinkable. When they weren't trying to kill him, they were trying to embarrass him. One idea was to put a noxious chemical in his shoes which would cause his trademark beard to fall out.

WAR PLAN RED

Declassified reports from government archives have revealed that the United States drew up plans on how to invade supposedly friendly countries, including Canada, before World War Two. In the 1920s, American spies were worried about the strength of the British Empire, leading them to invent what they dubbed "War Plan Red," in which they imagined that should the British want to attack the American capital, US forces would make pre-emptive attacks on Canadian ports and railway hubs in order to stop the UK using the country as a base for their invasion of Washington D.C. They theorised that once Canada was conquered, the British would sue for peace. The plan went as far as obtaining approval by the Defense Secretary, but when World War Two broke out, they decided they probably wouldn't need to fight the Canadians or the British. Nevertheless, they filed the plan away, just in case. Other secret reports exposed included War Plan Gold—a planned war with the French and their colonies in the Caribbean—and War Plan Indigo, which covered a possible invasion of Iceland.

UNWANTED MONEY

A billion dollars are waiting at the Federal Reserve, but nobody wants them. The American government would like US citizens to swap their beloved dollar bill for a dollar coin in order to save money, as metal coins don't wear out like paper bills. So they have been producing millions of freshly minted coins ready for the surge in demand. The problem is that nobody wants them. All these coins, which cost more than $300 million to mint, are languishing in storage at the Federal Reserve because most people would rather use good old banknotes.

OPERATION NORTHWOODS

Sometimes conspiracy theories are more real than you think. Declassified documents from the 1960s have revealed that high-ranking American defense officials developed a plan to shoot down a civilian airliner. The idea was to blame it on Cuba in a so-called "false flag" attack, in order to justify a declaration of war on the communist country and gain US public support.

Other plans included blaming Cuba if the 1962 space flight manned by John Glenn happened to crash, by planting evidence of electronic interference from the communists, and mounting covert attacks on other countries and blaming the Cubans, in order to gain the support of other nations for military retaliation. The report got as far as President Kennedy, who didn't waste any time in vetoing it.

THE ARMY OF APES

Joseph Stalin had some bizarre plans when he was leader of the Soviet Union. He was inspired by the ideas of controversial biologist Ilya Ivanov, who had long claimed that it was possible to mate humans with other animals to create hybrid creatures—his favorite being a human crossed with an ape. The notion caught Stalin's imagination and he ordered the experiments to start. The plan was to breed an invincible army of human-ape soldiers that would have the strength of a gorilla and the brain of a man, and could be ordered to do anything on the battlefield.

Stalin gave Ivanov free rein to travel to Africa for his research, where he captured specimens to take back to Russia for his experiments at a secret laboratory. Firstly, he impregnated female gorillas, chimpanzees and orang-utans with human sperm, and waited for them to conceive. When this failed, he asked for human volunteers to be impregnated with primate sperm and, incredibly, several loyal Soviet women did offer their services.

His cruel experiments failed to yield a human-ape child, and after a few years he suffered the same fate as many of Stalin's favorites. He was arrested and sent to a labor camp, where he quickly died. Many years later, builders working on a site in present-day Georgia dug up many bones in a mass grave: they had uncovered the location of Ivanov's secret laboratory. The bones were identified as the remains of the unfortunate apes that had been part of his experiments.

ONE OF OUR MISSILES IS MISSING

Given the dangerous and sensitive nature of the world's nuclear weapons stockpile, you would be forgiven for thinking that we know exactly how many warheads a country has, and where they are, at any one time. That's not always the case. Several nuclear warheads have been lost by the United States, and nobody knows their whereabouts. Security experts have admitted to being concerned over the location of the bombs, as decades later they may still be functioning should rogue states or terrorist organizations get their hands on them.

In 1950 a B-36 bomber on a training mission developed engine trouble, forcing the crew to detonate their 30-kiloton nuclear bomb, with twice the explosive power of the explosion over Hiroshima in 1945, over the Pacific Ocean. Fortunately, the bomb was not fitted with the plutonium core necessary for a nuclear explosion. Six years later, a bomber carrying two nuclear weapons disappeared in bad weather over the Mediterranean. The whereabouts of the plane, and its payload, remain a mystery. When a B-52 broke up soon after take-off over North Carolina in 1961, two 4-megaton nuclear bombs—each more than 250 times as powerful as the 1945 Hiroshima detonations—were ejected from the plane and fell to earth. One of the devices deployed a parachute and landed safely in a tree; the other plunged so deeply into the muddy ground that only fragments were recovered. In 1965 a plane fell off an aircraft carrier and was lost in deep waters in the Pacific Ocean, along with the hydrogen bomb on board.

In 1968 a US bomber carrying four nuclear missiles crashed into ice in Greenland. The conventional explosives detonated, spreading radioactive material over the area, but luckily the nuclear warheads were not armed, so a full-scale nuclear blast was averted. A thorough recovery mission only retrieved fragments from three of the bombs; it's thought that the fourth is still somewhere buried under the ice, waiting to be discovered.

OPERATION KUWAITI FIELD CHICKEN

In the build-up for the US-led invasion of Iraq, the Americans were worried, as they marched on Baghdad, about the Iraqis deploying chemical weapons against them, so they planned to use chickens as early-warning gas detectors. The birds would be kept in cages on top of armored cars, and if they died, the soldiers would don their protective equipment, in much the same way as canaries were once taken down mines to warn workers of toxic gases.

The plan was dubbed Operation Kuwaiti Field Chicken, or KFC for short, and engineers from the tank division were tasked with buying up hens in Kuwaiti markets to use in the field. The plan hit a roadblock after 95 per cent of the chickens died of heat exhaustion on arrival in the roasting hot desert and were eaten, KFC-style, by the soldiers. The missing chickens were replaced by pigeons that were better suited to withstand such high temperatures.

Chickens were used in a similar capacity during the first Gulf War and one morning a troop woke up to find all of them dead. They scrambled for their gas masks, thinking that there must have been a chemical attack, but it turned out that the unfortunate fowls had simply frozen to death when the desert temperature plummeted overnight. These chickens also came in handy in the mess tent later that day.

THE TWO-HEADED DOG

In 1959, *Life* magazine ran a shocking story on the latest scientific experiment from the Soviet Union: the quest to create a two-headed dog. The bizarre procedure was part of long-term research into the transplantation of human organs, something which might seem commonplace now but that at the time was only in its infancy. The man in charge of the operation was Dr Vladimir Demikhov, who wanted to splice the head and fore legs from a small nine-year-old dog called Shavka onto the side of the neck of a larger stray shepherd dog, called Palma. The latter had already received an extra heart at the hands of Demikhov.

The two unsuspecting dogs were put under anesthetic and shaved. Shavka's body was sliced in half, and the main blood vessels were carefully attached to the vessels in the larger dog's neck. Her head was tied onto Palma's body and the skin stitched together. The cruel procedure took just three and a half hours to complete, and witnesses reported that, not long after the operation, both dogs were happily lapping at a bowl of water.

The experiment did not take long because Demikhov had had plenty of practice; the two dogs were victims of the twenty-fourth experiment to create a two-headed canine, all of which eventually died. Shavka and Palma succumbed after four days, but others had lasted for a month. Worryingly, Demikhov told journalists that this was only the start and that he planned to begin experimenting with human subjects. Asked where he would source the raw materials, he replied that Moscow had more than enough dead people to provide the organs that he needed.

Eight years later, the first human heart transplant was performed in South Africa, by a surgeon who had replicated the dog experiments, after seeing a photograph in the newspaper, and had visited Demikhov's lab for advice.

HUNGARY vs GOLIATH

In 1961 a fin whale carcass more than 20 metres long and weighing almost 70 tons was loaded onto a lorry and driven around the streets of Hungary. The unusual traveller was said to be part of a Cold War intrigue involving nuclear weapons and espionage. The bizarre cargo, called Goliath, and two other fin whales caught by Norwegian whalers in the 1950s toured Europe as an educational attraction, wowing huge crowds who had never seen such a monster up close. They were also intended as a way to promote the whaling industry to post-war Europe.

But when Goliath made it beyond the Iron Curtain into Soviet Hungary, the problems started. The whale made such an impression that the tour was mentioned in Hungarian books and films for years afterwards. Everybody was talking about it, and some thought that the great marine mammal was actually part of a Western plot to undermine the communist system. Why else was this Western capitalist attraction touring in the East?

Citizens who lived under the Soviet Union regime were bombarded with anti-Western propaganda on a regular basis, and rumors of such plots were rife. The previous decade, the East German authorities had claimed that Western powers had caused a potato shortage by dropping thousands of Colorado potato beetles—a pest that can cause huge damage to crops—from planes flying over farms. Newspapers reported several incidents in which farmers had seen American planes flying overhead and then discovered an infestation of bugs in their potatoes. The government described the act as "a criminal attack by American imperialist warmongers on our people's food supply," and East German children were enlisted to patrol fields and catch potato beetles.

When Goliath made its appearances in Hungary, the nuclear arms race was well under way, and citizens lived in fear of attack and invasion. It was claimed that the great weight and outsize dimensions of the bizarre cargo were comparable to those of the large missile carriers developed by the Americans—and that the journey was not to promote whaling, but to test whether the road network behind the Iron Curtain could handle such loads, in preparation for an invasion from the West. The truth behind Goliath's trip may never be exposed.

FLYING SAUCERS

Secret files declassified by the United States government have revealed that the US Air Force once began work on a genuine flying saucer. The detailed plans from the 1950s revealed a search for a new aircraft that could take off from remote airfields, travel at supersonic speeds and fly at high altitude in order to combat

Russian bombers. They dreamt up a contraption that looked more like something from outer space: capable of hovering in the air, reaching speeds of more than 3,000 mph and ascending to 100,000 feet. The saucer was surprisingly small—about 20 feet in diameter—and was powered by six jet engines. The official government line is that when the first prototypes were constructed, they barely made it off the ground, so the project was canned and classified. The discovery led aviation experts to wonder what other strange machines the government might have been working on, extraterrestrial or otherwise, and others even went as far as linking the flying saucer prototypes to the famous alien sighting at Roswell the previous decade.

BIRD BOMBS

Secret government files released in 2004 revealed that in the 1950s the British Army developed a nuclear bomb that relied on chickens to keep it working. The warhead was designed to be buried underground in European countries considered vulnerable to Soviet invasion and detonated in the event this actually happened. As many of these places had freezing winters, the scientists worried that the sensitive bomb would malfunction. So they came up with the idea of burying colonies of live poultry with the warhead, as the heat emanating from them would help to keep the unstable device at the correct operating temperature.

Incredibly, this wasn't the only "bird bomb" to have been invented by Western powers. Pigeons are remarkably good at recognising objects, with one study revealing that they can differentiate between artworks painted by Monet and Picasso. Documents unearthed in the American national archives exposed a design for a pigeon-guided explosive, giving a new meaning to the term "smart bomb." A conventional bomber plane would drop the bomb, and brave pigeons, trained for several weeks at secret facilities with food rewards, would direct the weapon to its target by pecking at controls with their beaks. The bombs had lenses in the nose cone, which would project objects on the ground onto a screen in front of the birds. They were trained to peck when they recognized a target on the screen, directing the trajectory of the explosives. Sadly, it was a one-way flight.

BAT BOMBS

The American government once seriously considered using bats in warfare. Bat bombs were the brainchild of eccentric inventor Lytle S. Adams—an associate of First Lady Eleanor Roosevelt—who developed the dastardly idea to repay the Japanese for the 1941 attack on Pearl Harbor. His plan involved fitting individual bats with miniature incendiary bombs and letting them loose over Japan. They would soon destroy entire cities by following their natural instinct to hide under bridges, and in the nooks and crannies of buildings, which in Japan were still largely constructed of wood and paper, and therefore particularly vulnerable to fire.

Always keen on new ideas in the desperate fight against the Axis powers, and perhaps because of Adams's friendship with the President's wife, the United States Army decided to put the idea to the test, stating their confidence in the plan with the immortal phrase, "This man is not a nut."

Thousands of tiny Mexican free-tailed bats were captured in nets and shipped inside refrigerated ice-cube trays. This lowered their body temperature so that they would go into hibernation mode for their journey to the front line. Then the bats were fitted with small incendiary bombs on timers and placed inside bomb casings, which would be dropped from planes and open up mid-flight, allowing them to escape and find somewhere to roost, before exploding in flames and hopefully bringing a building down with them.

The ingenious idea did not work as well as the Army had hoped. The exploding bats managed to escape and find a perfect roost inside an American Air Force hangar, destroying the building and several planes. Nevertheless, both the Navy and the Marine Corps persevered with bat bomb testing, spending in the region of $2 million before the race for the atomic bomb meant that the project was mothballed. Adams always maintained that the bats would have been preferable to the horrors wrought by the hydrogen bombs that finally ended the war.

OLD GLORY

You have probably never even noticed the metal ball on top of flagpoles flying the Stars and Stripes flag in the United States, so you probably never wondered what was inside it. Each ball, which can be seen atop flagpoles on all official federal and state buildings, contains the same thing: a box of matches and a bullet. The story behind the unusual objects dates back to the early years of the Cold War, when paranoia about communist sympathisers in the States was at its peak. The idea was that if the town, state or country suffered an invasion, the last surviving American soldier would find his way to the flag and perform a sacred duty. The matches were for him to burn the flag, so that the enemy couldn't get their hands on it, and the bullet was to shoot himself, so that they couldn't get their hands on him either—or perhaps out of shame at having destroyed Old Glory. Obviously, now that the Cold War has ended, it's extremely unlikely that any such event would occur, but the tradition has remained. The government won't confirm or deny the story, but many servicemen believe it's true. Some say that the ball, known as a "truck" in military circles, contains food, too, so that the soldier will have enough energy to complete his task. It's also rumored that the finial at the top of the regimental colors carried by military flag bearers contains similar implements, although this is now merely ceremonial, as flags are no longer carried into battle.

ANIMALS

EATS LIKE A PIG

One day a farmer from Oregon went to feed his pigs, just as he did every morning but, on this particular occasion, he never returned. When his family became concerned, they went to look for him at the farm, but there was nobody there. Then they looked in the enclosure where the man kept his beloved pigs, some of which tipped the scales at more than 300 kilos. Something in the muck caught their eye: it was a pair of dentures. When they looked more closely, they could see pieces of meat strewn around the pigsty and they soon realized what had happened: the pigs had eaten their owner.

Pigs might seem like characterful creatures that like their human keepers, but they are also known to eat anything that is put in front of them, happily crunching through bones without difficulty. It's not a coincidence that gangsters and serial killers often talk of feeding victims to pigs in movies, as that farmer found to his cost. Investigators discovered that one of the sows had bitten the man on another occasion, after he accidentally trod on one of her piglets, but he had decided not to kill the offending animal.

Was this a tragic accident or an act of revenge? It's possible that the giant pigs knocked the farmer over and then decided he was pig food—or he may have suffered a medical emergency. The truth will never come out: there was not enough left of him to determine the cause of death.

SUICIDE BRIDGE

A couple were out walking their pet sheepdog on a bright sunny morning around an ancient Scottish estate. The walk was unremarkable until they started to cross an old stone bridge spanning a rocky river, and the dog suddenly became agitated.

One of the creepiest spots in all of Scotland is the Overtoun Bridge, site of a great many tragedies over the years. It's said that something in the air causes otherwise sane minds to go mad when they walk across the bridge, and leap to their deaths in the river 50 feet below. However, these minds are not those of humans, but those of their dogs, who are not aware of the danger below, as the walls are generally too high for them to be able to see over the side. There have been more than 50 reports of pet dogs inexplicably leaping to their deaths from the bridge since the 1950s so authorities have warned dog owners not to visit the picturesque valley, or at least to make sure that they keep their pets on a short lead.

There are clear links between the incidents: they always happen in good weather and all the dogs leap off the same side of the bridge. Also, the episodes tend to involve dogs with long snouts, leading some to believe that those with a strong chase instinct are smelling something in the air that causes them to jump into the valley, perhaps disorientated. One pet that survived the jump was said to be so shocked that all its hair fell out. Some have speculated that the estate, which features an old house, is haunted. Another theory is that the river below is popular with populations of wild mink escaped from fur farms and it's their smell that drives the canines wild.

UNDERGROUND GATORS

A popular tale—or should that be "tail"—that has been circulating since before World War Two concerns the possible inhabitants of New York's labyrinthine sewer network. Various newspapers have reported alligators being tracked in the sewers, usually identified as unwanted pets.

Supposedly, tourists visiting Florida, where the alligators are found in the wild, would buy young reptiles as pets but when they realized that their growing gators were no longer that cute—and would soon outgrow the bath—they flushed them down toilets and drains.

If the alligators survived this ordeal, they grew fat on the thousands of sewer rats, which weren't expecting to find an apex predator round the next corner, and mated with each other to create a subterranean reptile swamp. The first reported sightings emerged in the 1930s, when sewer workers caught flashes of the creatures in their flashlights, and hunters prowled the tunnels armed with rifles. In 1935 the *New York Times* reported that youths shovelling snow into a manhole had spotted an 8-foot-long gator in the water at the bottom of the drainpipe. He was extricated and killed. Some say that sewer gators go blind and lose their color due to the lack of sunlight, like other known reptiles that live in complete darkness.

Stories of these reptiles growing to unprecedented proportions due to the effects of noxious chemicals in the drains are particularly unsettling. Alligators have long been known to travel through storm drains in Southern American states, often emerging in suburban neighborhoods, thus proving that they can survive in these environments.

TROUSER SNAKES

While alligators might make their way into the sewers via a toilet, you might see snakes coming through in the opposite direction. At least, you'd better hope you see them, before they see you. An Israeli man was bitten in a sensitive area by a snake, reportedly small and non-venomous, but still terrifying, which had slithered through a drainpipe and into his toilet while he was sitting on it. If that wasn't frightening enough, much larger snakes have reportedly made surprise appearances in the bathroom. In Singapore an 8-foot-long python is known to have bitten a man on another important body part while he was minding his own business on the bowl. In Australia, a python in the potty is no longer considered newsworthy, perhaps unsurprisingly, as specimens up to 10 feet in length are known to slide their way into people's houses looking for a drink, while other snakes have been reported in American bathrooms from Pennsylvania to San Diego.

SEWER RATS

Even if you live in a country that doesn't suffer from infestations of alligators or snakes, you are still not safe. In any major city you are probably at risk from coming across another unwanted visitor in the bathroom. A woman in South London was bitten by a rat that tried to jump out of her toilet while she was still sitting on it. To her horror she looked into the bowl and saw several other rodents trying to escape, and they weren't put off by repeated flushes. She used a toilet plunger to plug the hole until pest controllers arrived to sort out the problem.

In another incident in the same area, a couple heard a strange scratching sound coming from under the toilet seat and opened it to find a rat trying to get out of the bowl. Rats can hold their breath for long periods and squeeze through the tiniest of gaps; they find it easy to shimmy up drainage pipes from city sewers into toilets in search of food and whatever else people flush down toilets. In America toilet rats are particularly attracted by the food disposal systems in kitchen sinks, with sightings spanning from Seattle to New York.

DOG FOOD

A French woman was out for dinner with friends and returned late in the evening to her house in the suburbs. Usually, she would expect to see her devoted Rottweiler dog waiting at the front door, but on this occasion he did not come to greet her, which made her nervous, as she lived on her own. She then heard a strange noise coming from the kitchen: the dog was there, but he was having trouble breathing and making terrible choking noises. She rushed over to her pet, who was lying on his bed, a look of panic on his face. She loaded him into the car with some difficulty and drove to the vet.

As her pet was wheeled into the procedure room, she told the vet that the dog often ate things that he shouldn't; in fact, he would scoff anything he could get his jaws around. The vet inserted a tube into the dog's throat so that the animal could breathe and told the owner not to worry; she could return home for the night and would receive a phone call once the issue had been investigated further.

As she was walking through her front door, the vet rang. The dog was fine, but the owner needed to get to a neighbor's house immediately and call the police. The vet had found the remains of a freshly severed human hand inside the dog, obstructing his airway, and an X-ray revealed finger bones in the stomach. When the police arrived, they found an intruder in the back garden, passed out from blood loss after losing a hand to a Rottweiler.

NUCLEAR COCKROACHES

If we suffered a nuclear apocalypse, would cockroaches really be left walking the earth? These creatures have lasted on our planet for more than 300 million years and are notoriously tough—so tough that it's often said that they would be able to survive in conditions in which humans would perish. However, while cockroaches would outlive us in the event of nuclear winter, they would still eventually die. Humans are ten times more sensitive to the effects of radiation, but a nuclear explosion would far exceed the levels that even a cockroach could survive. Other creatures with less of a reputation may fare rather better, though. The parasitic wasp *Habrobracon* is incredibly resistant to radiation, able to withstand levels 500 times stronger than those which would kill a human. It's estimated that the wasp could survive even after being exposed to nuclear blasts many times more powerful than the bombs dropped on Japan at the end of World War Two. But given that the modern nuclear arsenal is several powers of magnitude higher than those detonations, even parasitic wasps may perish. The only creatures that could be guaranteed to be roaming a scorched earth ravaged by nuclear fallout are the incredibly hardy bacteria that can be found at the bottom of the sea. They can withstand radiations 7,500 times stronger than those which would kill a human. But you won't find them in your kitchen cupboards.

SLATS THE LION

Everybody is familiar with the roaring MGM lion that appears at the start of old black-and-white movies but not everyone knows the true story behind the big cat. There were actually several different lions used over the years. The first one had to be "retired" after an incident during filming. In the 1920s MGM hired a lion called Slats from an Irish animal trainer to be filmed for the logo. He wasn't supposed to roar, only look at the camera in silence. When working with animals, however, things don't always go to plan. The story goes that two burglars happened upon the shoot and Slats went mad, roaring at the intruders, killing one of them and seriously injuring the other before his trainer could pull him off. The cameras caught Slats's roar on film, and this was used instead. From then on all the MGM lions had to roar.

PET CEMETERY

A police officer lived on a small estate where everybody knew each other. He was watching television one day when he noticed his terrier chewing at something in the corner of the kitchen: the place where the pet took things he knew he wasn't supposed to eat. It was something furry. The owner took it from the dog's reluctant jaws and realized with a grimace that it was a bunny rabbit, very dead, probably taken from the fields beyond his garden. However, he soon recognized this particular bunny. It wasn't wild: it was the prize-winning specimen from his next-door neighbor's garden. The man was horrified and felt extremely guilty, particularly as he knew the neighbor, Ted, very well. The rabbit's neck was broken, but there were no other visible injuries, so this gave him an idea. He cleaned the dog slobber off the rabbit and put it in a bag in his fridge. Then he waited until it was dark, sneaked over the garden fence and placed the rabbit carefully back in its hutch, hoping that his neighbor would assume it had died of natural causes.

Later that week he was talking to Ted, who mentioned the rabbit's death and also that there was something very strange going on. The dog owner started to feel extremely guilty and hoped it didn't show. The neighbor explained that he didn't believe in superstitions or any such nonsense, but the rabbit affair had left him puzzled. Ted described how he had found the rabbit dead inside the locked hutch.

"That's a shame," replied the policeman. "I know how you loved that rabbit."

"Yes, but that's not the weird part," the neighbor went on. "He had died the day before. I had already buried him in the flower bed!"

BONSAI CATS

In the year 2000 a mysterious website appeared online where a Japanese man claimed to be selling unique kittens that he called "Bonsai cats." He described how he bred the creatures by applying the same techniques that the Japanese used for their famous miniature Bonsai trees. The kittens were sealed inside small glass tubes when they were very young, and their bodies would grow moulded by the tubes in whatever shape the owner preferred. When the kittens reached adult age, the tube was removed, revealing a unique form. Like other house cats, they stayed indoors, so they didn't need to be as functional as a regular pet.

As the site declared, "You no longer need be satisfied with a house pet having the same mundane shape as all other members of its species." The process started with kittens being drugged to relax their muscles, before being eased into the tube. The young cats were given food through a tube, and waste products were removed through another tube. Bonsai kittens were reportedly popular amongst wealthy cat lovers in New York and Asia, particularly those living in high-rise apartments.

If this sounds like an outrageously cruel method of breeding fashionable pets, don't fret, because the website was a hoax. A very convincing hoax, however, which provoked so much outrage around the world that the site was investigated by the FBI. They apparently found no evidence of anything illegal going on, so the bizarre site was left up on the web.

A REPTILE'S REVENGE

When an Oklahoma boy died only hours after complaining of a badly swollen foot, the doctors at the hospital were stumped. He had shown all the signs of a venomous snake bite, presenting with anxiety, vomiting and a raging fever, and then his heart had given out. However, before he lost consciousness, he said that he did not remember seeing a snake, never mind being bitten by one, and that he had been at home when he fell ill. They learned that the boy's father had also died of a snake bite the previous year, but that wasn't a mystery: he had killed a snake found under his truck in the desert and received a bite in the process.

A post-mortem on the boy revealed conclusively that his death was caused by rattlesnake venom, and an investigation was launched. A search of his house turned up no leads but then his brother was rushed to hospital a few months later with exactly the same symptoms. This time the doctors were ready, and the boy survived after they administered antivenom. Incredibly, he didn't have any idea how he had been "bitten" by the invisible snake either, until he mentioned that he'd been wearing his brother's snakeskin boots. There had to be a link. Upon examination, they saw that hidden in the toe was a rattlesnake fang. The boys' mother had made the boots out of the rattler that killed their father and, many years later, the fang in the toe had threatened one life and taken another in revenge.

A NEW DOG

An American couple travelled to Mexico on vacation. They were staying in a small town by the sea, notable for the large amount of small stray dogs that used to follow tourists around. They knew they were a soft touch and would feed them snacks. One of these dogs, an unusual-looking mongrel puppy of unknown breeding, followed the couple all the way back to their apartment and waited outside the front door all night. They took pity on it and the wife decided to smuggle it back across the border in their car; she already had a cat but had always wanted a puppy. The little dog grew quickly when they returned to America and soon dwarfed the other pet in the house. One day the woman returned home from work to find her cat dead in the kitchen, killed by a wound to the neck. She found the new dog cowering in the corner, with blood on its jaws and bad scratches to its face. She assumed that whatever had killed the cat had attacked the dog as well, so she took the dog to the vet to have its wounds treated and soon received a phone call. The creature she had adopted was not a stray Mexican dog; it was an abnormally large sewer rat—an aggressive invasive species—that would have to be put to sleep.

WHERE IT RAINS FISH

South America is known for some extreme weather, but in the town of Yoro, in Honduras, it regularly rains fish. Each spring, for as long as anyone can remember, thunderstorms cause thousands of fish to rain down from the sky. The unfortunate fish are not native to local lakes and rivers, and Yoro is 50 miles from the ocean, meaning that one explanation—that tornados are sucking the fish from the water and depositing them on land—is unlikely. One oddity is that the fish are nearly all blind, leading some to suggest that they are not coming from the sky at all, but underground rivers. Residents believe that the bizarre weather started after a Spanish missionary arrived in the nineteenth century. He prayed for God to provide the locals with food, as Jesus had fed the 5,000, and each year He obliges.

DANGEROUS DOLPHINS

If you're ever swimming in the Gulf of Mexico and you come across a friendly looking dolphin, don't get too close—it might have a licence to kill. In the 1980s the US Navy began training dolphins and sea lions as undercover operatives. Fitted with electrical sensors that their handlers used to control them, the mammals were deployed to detect mines in ports, keep watch for enemy divers around nuclear submarines in ports and help to protect warships at sea.

When Hurricane Katrina devastated the Gulf of Mexico in 2005, a story began circulating that a pod of these highly trained and intelligent creatures had escaped into the sea from a facility on the coast of Louisiana. Even more frightening were the rumors that these particular cetaceans were trained not just to patrol, but to kill. After a US warship was targeted by terrorists in a harbor in Yemen in the 1990s, the US Navy apparently started to train their dolphins for more aggressive missions, fitting them with toxic dart guns to shoot at underwater intruders. The government refused to confirm or deny reports that the animals were missing. Dolphin experts expressed concern that the escaped animals may have been conditioned to attack divers in wetsuits in naval training exercises, and that they would not be able to tell the difference between a terrorist and a regular swimmer. Luckily, nobody ever reported meeting the combat cetaceans—or at least, nobody survived to tell the tale.

Before their success with dolphins, the US Navy tried to harness the powers of larger sea mammals. They wanted to train pilot whales and orcas to follow boats out to sea and also to retrieve items, such as explosives, from the sea floor at depths that human divers could never hope to match. In the late 1960s a male orca, called Ishmael after the *Moby Dick* character, was captured off the coast of Washington State and trained in California before being transferred for open-sea testing in Hawaii. On his first mission "off the leash," as it were, out of his sea pen, he was conditioned to return when called via a radio transmitter attached to his head. After several hours of retrieving items, Ishmael apparently got bored of the tests, slapped his great tail on the water near the observing boat and swam off into deep water. He ignored the radio messages calling him back and was never seen again.

TOPSY THE ELEPHANT

Sometimes technological progress can be cruel. In the early twentieth century, electricity innovator Thomas Edison was keen to prove that his direct current system (DC) was much safer than the alternating current (AC) promoted by his inventor rival Nikola Tesla. Supporters of DC attempted to demonstrate the danger of AC by electrocuting several stray dogs in public. They administered several high-voltage shocks using DC, which the animals survived, and then killed them with AC shocks. The backers of alternating current were not convinced by this, as dogs were much smaller than human beings, so Edison's company had to think bigger, electrocuting several calves and then a horse. Even these demonstrations did not decide the battle of the currents.

Then came the news that a New York zoo wanted to get rid of Topsy, a female Asian elephant, after she was held responsible for the deaths of several zoo workers. Edison's men suggested that instead of the planned hanging, Topsy should be electrocuted— using Tesla's AC current, of course. The experiment was a success, and after being strangled with ropes and fed poisoned carrots,

Topsy was finished off by the powerful alternating current. Despite going to all this trouble, Edison failed in his fight against alternating current, which is now the industry standard.

MURDEROUS MARY

Incredibly, Topsy was not the last elephant to be sent to death row in America.

"Murderous Mary" was an Asian elephant weighing 5 tons that performed with the Sparks brothers' circus in the early twentieth century. Her story is a tragic indictment of the way that old-fashioned circuses used to treat wild animals. Mary was the star of the show, and her owners whipped up excitement about her in local newspapers by spreading rumors that she had killed several people.

One day in 1916 she finally lived up to her fearsome billing, turning on her trainer in front of a crowd. She grabbed him with her trunk, threw him to the ground and crushed his head with her foot, killing him instantly. A large audience had come to see Mary's performance that day, but instead they began to chant for her death. It was later revealed that the trainer was a vagrant who had been hired only days before, and knew nothing about handling exotic animals of Mary's size. He had been hitting her with a stick while she was trying to eat a watermelon. The elephant reportedly suffered from a painful tooth abscess, which may also have explained her aggression.

However, the reason why Mary killed the man was not immediately important: the circus needed to do something to entertain the crowd who had come to see the star of the show. They announced that Mary should be executed for her crime; they could make a show of it. They struggled to dispose of the great beast, however, as the bullets from several large-calibre guns failed to make an impact. Eventually, they hired a 100-ton derrick crane, tied a chain around Mary's neck, and she was hanged to death in front of 2,500 people.

THE STALLION

An old horse trainer from Ireland, who was close to retirement, was pressured to bring an old champion to the races to make up the numbers. He had gradually sold all of his horses until he only had old nags and one old racehorse left, whom he hadn't run for a few years. He needed the money, so reluctantly he went out to the retired horse's paddock to fetch him. He dragged his rusty old horse trailer out of the barn; it was looking a bit worse for wear, but the journey wasn't a long one.

He led the horse to the trailer, but the creature seemed to know that something was wrong and refused to be pulled up the ramp. The man, who usually trusted the instincts of his horses, decided to ignore the animal's protests and, although he knew it was the wrong thing to do, he chucked a carrot into the trailer, pushed him in and shut the door. The stallion stamped his feet and made a racket, but the man was already starting the truck and pulling out of the yard. The trailer creaked and shuddered, and the poor horse protested all the way. As the man pulled out onto the main road, he heard a terrible whinnying. People in other cars were overtaking and trying to bring his attention to the horse in distress, but the old trainer knew that the stallion had never liked travelling in the trailer and concentrated instead on the fact that he wasn't far from the racecourse.

Finally, he pulled into the paddock and went to check on the horse, when he saw a trail of blood reaching back to the road. The horse must have sustained an injury, he thought—the last thing he needed—and he rushed to open the doors. What he saw next he would never forget. After years of neglect, the wooden floor of the trailer had rotted, and when the horse had kicked up a fuss, his legs had fallen straight through and scraped along the road. By the time they had reached the racecourse, they were ground down to bloody stumps, and the poor horse was dead. The man was ruined: he had to sell his farm to pay his bills and legal costs.

WATCH WHAT YOU EAT

FOREIGN FOOD

Smalec, or lard, is a popular Polish product, usually eaten spread on slices of bread, like butter. It's so popular that some people make their own; but if you ever visit, you might want to ask exactly where it came from and what it contains. A Polish woman who kept a large number of dogs on a farm was arrested after it was discovered that she was overfeeding the animals to plump them up, before killing them and draining their body fat to make smalec. In rural parts of Poland the fat from canines has long been thought to have particular health benefits, so that is how she marketed her special brand of smalec, which she claimed to have taken every evening with her dinner and which she sold for £30 per pint. When authorities raided the premises, they found cages full of dogs—some of which were too fat to walk—and a slaughterhouse containing a fridge packed with bottles of fat.

SNAKE SOUP

A Chinese chef in a backstreet restaurant in Shanghai, where all manner of unusual delicacies—such as frogs, scorpions and other creepy-crawlies—were served, was preparing that night's special: king cobra soup. He had cooked it a hundred times before and always took precautions, as the dish required a freshly killed cobra. He removed the hissing reptile carefully from a cage, holding it just behind the head, and decapitated it as quickly as he could, being careful to avoid the venomous fangs. At the end of the night, as he was clearing up, the chef saw that he had forgotten to throw the head away. As he picked it up to throw it in the bin, he felt a sharp pain and saw that the fangs had sunk into his hand. He was dead before antivenom could be administered. Remember that even a dead snake can inflict a deadly bite.

CAT FOOD

You've probably heard about people eating dogs and cats in parts of China and Korea, but what about closer to home? Animal rights activists have started an online petition to get Switzerland to ban the eating of cats and dogs. Why is this necessary, you might ask? In certain rural parts of the country, eating pets is part of a long culinary tradition, and perfectly legal, although the sale of such meat is prohibited. According to the activists' campaign, as much as 3 per cent of the Swiss population regularly consumes meals of the canine or feline variety, particularly at Christmas time. Cat is traditionally cooked in a stew, and dog meat is made into sausages, or dried like jerky, and is associated with various health benefits.

BEER DRINKERS

The British are famous for their drinking, but Russia is surely the undisputed heavyweight when it comes to a reputation for drinking other nations under the table. In 2011 the country passed a landmark law that it hoped would curb the population's alcoholic tendencies. After much deliberation, the President signed a bill that officially recognized beer as an alcoholic drink. In a country where vodka is the national beverage, beer was regarded as little more than flavored water. In fact, any alcoholic drink under 10-per-cent proof was classified as food. It's not the first time that authorities have made an effort to reduce alcohol consumption. Gorbachev banned the sale of vodka before lunchtime, and then also had to ban the sale of perfume and aftershave in the morning, because alcoholics were drinking it until they could get their hands on their favorite tipple.

HYDROGEN BEER

In the bars of downtown Tokyo, where salarymen go to drown their sorrows after work in karaoke bars, a recent revolution in beer-making has got everyone's attention. A new generation of younger drinkers who were worried about the amount of carbon dioxide in their beverages prompted a local brewery to market hydrogen beer. This contains less than half the amount of CO_2 found in a regular beer, with those missing bubbles replaced with hydrogen gas. They swear that it tastes fresher and lighter, and there's an amusing side effect which is great for karaoke singers: similarly to what happens after inhaling helium, it makes you sound like Mickey Mouse. As hydrogen is lighter than air, it affects the way sound waves travel in the body, so the voice sounds different, making even the deepest male baritone sound like Mariah Carey.

The company behind the innovation has denied reports that the beer is dangerous, even though it is said that the beverage is shipped in custom-built boxes lined with metal to prevent an explosion from spreading in a confined space, and despite reports that it is highly flammable. Young men have been using cigarette lighters to spit hydrogen flames in bars across the city and putting the videos online. The company rejected claims that this was viral advertising and claimed it had nothing to do with them.

The company also denied that there is enough hydrogen gas in the beer to harm anyone, after a Tokyo insurance broker apparently seriously injured himself with the beer. According to his lawyer, the man lit a mouthful of hydrogen beer to pose for a photo and accidentally swallowed the flaming fluid. The brewery, however, blamed the broker's drunkenness for the incident, citing the owner of the bar, who stated in court that the broker had bought at least 20 bottles of hydrogen beer and drank ten of them—the rest he ignited in a series of explosions that terrorised the bar staff and left several with no eyebrows.

A BEAVER TALE

Next time you eat a raspberry ice cream, you might be able to thank a beaver for the taste. Castoreum is used as a sweet flavoring in raspberry and strawberry desserts, and also in perfume production. The substance is made from the secretions of the anal glands of the beaver, which the creature uses to mark its territory thanks to its powerful musky odor. Castoreum has been harvested throughout human history for use as fine incense, and in Roman times women would inhale the fumes in the belief that it worked as a form of birth control. For centuries people swore by its power for treating a wide range of ailments, which is perhaps not that far-fetched, as castoreum contains an active ingredient found in aspirin (beavers eat a lot of willow bark, where the drug originates). Although beavers used to be killed for their anal glands, these days they are captured humanely and the glands are "milked" for the smelly but useful secretion.

A GOOD VINTAGE

An English couple had recently invested in a wine-growing estate in the south of France, snapping it up for a cheap price at auction. The cellars were still full of hundreds of barrels of red wine and fine brandy—some of it drinkable, some of it less so. So they invited friends over from England for a party in the cellars to help them work out which ones to keep. As they opened barrel after barrel, they explained to their guests how they had managed to acquire the place at such a low price: the estate had been owned by a businessman who fled the country after being indicted for fraud, as he was caught laundering money through the winery.

As the evening wore on and everybody loosened up, they discovered an interesting old-looking brandy barrel, hidden in a vault deep in the basement. As they sampled the liquor, all of the guests commented on how expensive it tasted and guessed that the old owner probably didn't know how good it was. The next evening they returned again to fill up a bottle, but the brandy stopped pouring. They gave the barrel a shake, but it still refused to come. So they used a crowbar to lever the top off, even though that meant having to drink all of it—surely there was nothing wrong with that? However, they didn't touch another drop, as they discovered the preserved remains of a man lodged inside the barrel; one of his fingers was stuck in the tap. He had been effectively pickled and had clearly been there for a number of years. After that, the estate rather lost its appeal. The couple eventually poured every barrel down the drain, sold up and moved back to England.

FRIGHTENING FOOD

A woman was driving home from work and was late to pick up her children from her estranged husband. She knew they would be hungry but there was no time to cook anything, so she pulled into a drive-through Mexican fast-food outlet and hurriedly ordered her usual batch of burritos. When she got home, the kids devoured the food without a second thought, but one of them complained that it tasted funny. The mother told her not to be fussy and that it would be wasteful not to finish what she had been given.

The next morning all of the children and their mother had terrible stomach ache, and when she later picked them up from school, they were all complaining of pains in their gums. When the symptoms did not ease, and their gums began to bleed, they visited the family dentist, who delivered some shocking news. The family were displaying the first signs of a cockroach infestation. The insects' eggs had burrowed into the gaps between their teeth and their gums, and were growing inside their mouths. The likely culprit was the fast food.

It turned out that the Food Standards Authority had recently shut the restaurant down because of their terrible hygiene record: there were rats in the deep fryers and insects in the refrigerators.

What the woman didn't realise was that some of the restaurant's employees had reopened the drive-through to make some extra money, without the boss knowing. With no rules, the kitchen had become dirtier than ever. When the Food Standards Authority raided the premises, they found one of the worst cockroach infestations they had ever seen, and the restaurant was never allowed to reopen.

UNCLE ROGER

A Dutch woman and her husband had moved to South Africa for a year. She had landed a new job in Cape Town, and her husband happened to have some elderly relatives in the region, including a kindly uncle called Roger. The couple liked their new country but they missed their home comforts, so the man's parents sent them food from Holland with their correspondence. The expats replied by posting South African delicacies like biltong and various obscure sausages.

One day the man's parents received a jar of powder in the post from South Africa, but the accompanying letter was missing and they assumed that it had got lost in the post, as it had to travel a long way to Europe. The jar was unlabelled, but they took it to be some kind of African flavoring, or perhaps an instant hot drink. It tasted strange, quite meaty, so they each had a mugful with hot water—they always thought they should try new things—and then left it in the cupboard. A couple of weeks later they received the missing letter. It said that the couple were having a great time abroad, but sadly Uncle Roger had died in his sleep. They had cremated him, and as one of his last wishes had been to return home to Holland, they had sent his ashes over in the parcel for his half-brother to spread on the canals where they grew up. There was nothing else in the parcel, and what had happened slowly dawned on them: they had made Uncle Roger into a disgusting hot drink, and the rest of him was sitting in the kitchen cupboard.

TRANSPORT

A GOOD TIP

A story was circulated online by a young college student from Ireland, who was driving home from work one evening when he saw a Mercedes stopped at the side of the road. An elderly man was hunched over one of the wheels, clearly having some trouble with a tyre wrench. The boy parked behind the broken-down vehicle and offered his services, as he was a bit of a petrolhead who had changed many wheels over the years. The man didn't seem terribly pleased with the offer, but he let the student help. While he was working, the young man complimented the owner on his choice of car and made jokes about his own vehicle, which he could barely afford to keep on the road. He liked to talk, and by the time the wheel was changed and the owner was ready to drive away, he had told him most of his life story. The driver had barely said a word until then, but he asked the student's name, thanked him and was on his way. A couple of weeks later, the student was going through his post one morning and opened an envelope. Inside was a cheque for £10,000, with a handwritten note saying that, hopefully, by the time he had finished college, he might be able to buy a Mercedes.

RUNAWAY TRAIN

In 1907 a brakeman working on a Mexican railway faced an impossible choice. His train had a full load of dynamite, so he had been driving extra carefully. He made a regular stop at a small-town station, when he noticed that the train's engine had problems and sparks were being blown from the chimney by the wind. That was concerning, given what he was carrying, but the wagons were covered. Then the worst happened: some straw on top of a wagon had caught fire from the sparks and fire took hold on the roof, fanned by the wind. He knew it was only a matter of time before his cargo did what it was designed to do, and there was no hope of putting the fire out. He could either flee, leaving it to explode in a built-up area, or take care of it himself. He decided to save the life of everybody in the town by firing up the engine and powering the train out into the desert as fast as it would go. A few miles out of town the inevitable happened, blowing the brakeman and the train sky-high in a massive explosion. For his selfless act of bravery, the town was renamed in his honor.

THE ABBEY

Many years ago a bus driver was working the night shift on a Sunday night in a British city. He was driving an empty double-decker bus on his usual route from the city out to the suburbs, when he saw something unusual. On his journey he passed an old ruined abbey, home to the largest cemetery in the city, but there was never anyone at that bus stop, for there were no houses on that road. However, that night there was someone waiting for the bus: a grey-haired man standing as if to attention at the side of the road.

The driver couldn't remember the last time he had picked somebody up at that stop; in fact, he initially drove past the man, before noticing him in his mirrors. He sighed and reversed back to the stop to pick him up. The man was smiling, which struck the driver as odd, and told him that he wished to go to the "next stop, please," before climbing up to the top deck without saying another word. Then the driver realized that the old gentleman hadn't bought a ticket, but he couldn't be bothered to stop and go upstairs; the man could pay before he got off.

The driver continued on his journey and completed the 20-minute stretch in surprisingly quick time. He stopped and waited for the man to come down, and when that didn't happen, he yelled that they had reached the stop he had asked for. There was no reply and the man did not appear, so the driver got out of his seat and peered up at the top deck. He walked up the steps and saw that there was nobody there; his passenger had disappeared. Was he imagining things? Then he heard the bus door open with a hiss. He looked back downstairs and saw that the smiling man was outside again, waiting at the bus stop. "What the—" the driver whispered to himself. He made as if to ask him what he was up to, but stopped when he saw the building behind the man. They were back at the abbey. "Next stop, please," said the man as he got on the bus.

LAST JOURNEY HOME

A young Italian man was travelling home from university at the end of term when a local family joined him in his carriage. Judging from their clothes, he assumed that they were rural workers; the mother started to chat to him about the long trip, while her husband sat next to her and their son next to him. They had carried the husband into the carriage, apologising and explaining that he'd been drinking too much wine. The man slumped with his cap over his face and didn't move. The son looked extremely embarrassed by the situation and smiled awkwardly at the student the whole time.

The mother never stopped talking, and the student eventually got the feeling that she was trying to distract him. When he leaned over the family to retrieve his trunk from the locker to get something out of it, she insisted that she lift the heavy case herself. Then the son left the carriage and the mother followed, saying that she would only be a minute. The student took the opportunity to put his case back in the locker, lifting it up over the man, but he lost his grip, and the case slipped through his hands and landed onto the man's head with a terrible crack. The man slumped to the floor, and the student gasped in horror at what he had done. All his attempts to wake him failed, and he started to worry that he'd killed the man. He felt for a pulse, but there was none.

The student started to panic and decided on his only option: he opened the carriage window and, with some difficulty, heaved the body out onto the tracks. Just as he closed the window, the woman returned. She stared at the empty seat with a worried look, but the student tried not to let on that anything had happened.

"Where is he?" the woman asked and the student calmly told her that he had gone off down the carriage, suggesting that perhaps he was in the restaurant car. The woman insisted that that was impossible and shook her finger in the boy's face, asking, "What have you done with him?" But he stuck to his story so the woman sat down, gathered herself and spoke to him calmly.

She explained that she wouldn't get the guard but the boy must help her to find her husband, who could not have possibly walked all the way to the restaurant car. "What makes you so sure?" the student asked. So she told him: "He was dead before he even got on the train." They were travelling to his funeral.

The boy sat in disbelief as the story was explained. The woman's husband had died the day before and in order to avoid the high cost of taking a coffin on the train, she had instead dressed him up in his usual clothes and pretended that he was a regular passenger. As the boy realized that he could no longer be classed as a murderer, he owned up to what he had done and the man was recovered from the tracks later that day. He was not in too bad a state and made it to his funeral.

THE RED MOTORBIKE

Jamie had wanted a motorbike for as long as he could remember. His uncle had one and gave him rides on the back until his mother had put a stop to it, saying it was too dangerous. He couldn't wait until he was old enough for his own bike, but first he would have to get round his mother, who hated the idea.

Jamie pestered his parents for months once he turned 16, and eventually they agreed to buy him one, but only if he got a good teacher and learned how to ride safely. His uncle agreed to show him the ropes and took him out on a few lessons. Jamie was a good student, and his uncle thought that he would soon be ready to go out on his own; he just needed to perform an emergency stop without falling off the bike, so he told his nephew to drive round the corner and then return. The uncle's plan was to jump off the pavement into Jamie's path, forcing him to brake as hard as he could. *No problem* thought the boy and disappeared out of sight. The uncle saw the red motorbike coming down the road and promptly jumped in front of it. However, the bike barely slowed down as it ploughed into him and threw him back onto the pavement, breaking several bones and leaving him unconscious. Seconds later, Jamie rode past, on an identical red motorbike.

BARN FIND

A remarkable tale of good fortune spread around the internet a few years ago. A New York City adman had retired after a long career in the office and wanted to spend his retirement funds wisely on a place in Portugal, where he and his wife had spent a vacation some years before, and where their money would go a bit further. They found a small farm with a modest house in a remote area, which, according to the agent, had been vacant for many years. There had been a few interested parties, but they had been put off by the isolated location and the presence of a very large unsightly barn that stood at the edge of the property, with large rusty doors welded shut. People assumed that the doors were needed to prevent squatters and that the barn was out of use. It would be expensive to tear it down, never mind to convert it into a usable building.

The New Yorkers made a low offer and took possession, putting the barn to the back of their minds until they moved in some months later. Finally, the adman thought that he should at least take a look inside the barn, so he hired a local to come and open the doors with an angle grinder. The barn looked even larger from the inside and was full of what looked like old farm machinery, covered in sheets thick with dust. Then he saw the glint of a wheel and realized that they were cars—very old cars—and there must have been more than 100 of them, packed in like sardines. Most specimens in this incredible collection were rusty wrecks—family saloons that were not really worth anything—but as he walked along the rows, he discovered ancient Bentleys, Ferraris, rare Porsches, Studebakers and the odd Rolls-Royce. The couple had stumbled upon the forgotten hoard of a reclusive and eccentric Portuguese collector who had died with no heirs and kept no record of his gigantic car collection. Nobody had ever bothered to look in the barn.

TRAGEDIES

THE HEARTBREAKER

A woman from a small town in England thought that she had lost everything when her husband was found dead. The investigation concluded that the man had taken his own life, but despite all the evidence, she was never convinced. They were happily married and he had just started a new job in a nearby town; he was a kind man who gave to charity and was on a list of organ donors. When a terribly ill man was given her husband's heart in a transplant, she took some solace that a little good had come of the tragedy.

She eventually met the man who had received her husband's heart and, against all her instincts, they struck up a relationship, marrying after a short courtship. She told friends that it was as if she had known him all her life. Life went on as usual for several years, until one Christmas Eve, when she returned from work late. She entered the house and a chill ran through her body, as old forgotten memories triggered in her mind. Her first husband had died at that time of year—in fact, five years to the day—and back then she had returned to find the same unexpected silence in the house. Then she heard the sound of water and saw it flowing down the stairs, tinged with red. It was exactly what she had seen on that night five years ago. She was scared and called out nervously for her husband, but there was no answer. She made her way up the stairs and saw the bloody liquid seeping from the bathroom—*not again*, she thought, it couldn't happen again...

THE LUCKY HARVEST

A ghostly fleet of fishing boats with a crew of dead fisherman aboard were discovered along the shores of Japan. More than 30 such vessels, all containing the decomposed remains of sailors, had drifted ashore. All the boats were made from wood and were in a terrible state of disrepair, which led the Japanese to wonder just how many similar vessels had sunk out at sea. Nobody knew where the boats came from, who was on board or what had happened to them on their fateful journeys. One theory was that the sailors were North Korean fisherman, who lost their bearings in a desperate bid to catch more fish, or unlucky defectors from the same country.

The grim discoveries brought to mind the well-known tale of a Japanese fishing vessel that ran into problems many years earlier, hundreds of miles out in the Pacific Ocean. An American coastguard boat first encountered the vessel—a fishing trawler called the *Lucky Harvest*—and received no reply when hailing it on their radio. They boarded her, suspicious that she may contain smugglers, and were shocked by what they found: the boat was only just afloat, with water rolling around the lower decks, and the engine room was flooded. On the top deck they found the bodies of three sailors, all in an advanced state of decomposition. In the wheelhouse there were more horrors: more bodies, some showing terrible injuries. A medic determined that some of the wounds had been inflicted after death.

The galley was stained with dry blood and covered with the remains of seabirds. As they investigated further, they discovered human bones in the oven and other horrors that the coastguard crew could not bear to include in their report. Fish bones were strewn all over the ship, and a foul stench arose from the cargo hold. They ascertained that the boat was Japanese registered and must have drifted thousands of miles before finding itself in American waters. It was last seen in its home port more than a year previously, before embarking on a tuna-fishing trip. Strangely, the boat's emergency radio was working, but no ships in the area had reported any distress calls. Then they found the ship's logbook, and to their horror saw that the last entry was dated only a few weeks before. Such details were pored over by investigators trying to determine what happened to the *Lucky Harvest*.

According to the log, the ship had developed engine troubles not long after leaving port, drifting into international waters while waiting for help to arrive. While trying to fix the engine, the crew found themselves at the mercy of a terrible storm, which lasted for a week. One night a gigantic wave hit the ship and rolled it upside down, and as water gushed into the wheelhouse, the crew thought they were doomed. Then, as if by magic, an even bigger wave crashed over the hull and righted the ship. Miraculously, everyone was accounted for.

When the storm cleared, they realized that they were thousands of miles from help and despite making several distress calls, there was no reply. The trawler nets were broken, so they could not catch any more fish. They worked out that with their previous catches, or what was left after the storm, they had only a few weeks' supply of food and little water, as their spare tanks had been washed overboard. For the first few days they held out hope of being rescued; they even spotted a couple of planes in the distance, but none flew over their position. They kept their spirits up by singing traditional fishermen's songs and occasionally, by some quirk, they were able to tune into mysterious radio stations.

The log reported that they spotted a container ship passing to the west. They were close enough to see that it was Chinese, but despite making more distress calls and shooting off their last flares, there was no response. By the end of the month, they were running out of fish and down to one container of water. They put tarpaulins and buckets out to catch any rain, but the skies refused to open. The captain had to break up a fight between two men who argued over water rations, and one sustained a serious head wound. They had nothing to treat him with, and he deteriorated quickly as it became infected. He was the first to die. Then they started catching seagulls with their bare hands, some of them eating the birds raw, which only made the men thirstier.

Hope turned into disaster when one of the sailors managed to catch a turtle. The men were turning delirious: the first mate swung an axe at the turtle catcher in a jealous rage, causing a fatal injury. Then the log entries became shorter and less frequent.

We are all losing hope, the bosun died today, we threw him overboard like the others. Our teeth are falling out. The cook is trying to survive by boiling leather and ropes to eat.

The cook is dead. I saw the mate cutting his arm off, we tried to stop him but we have no strength. This is our fate. When I awoke his body was nowhere to be seen.

The men are fighting over the dead like animals, I try to tell them that eating is no good if you have no water. I survive by sucking water from the eyes of rotting tuna.

I finished the last fish yesterday. I am the only one left now.

The account ends by telling how each of the men left locks of hair in the logbook for their families to remember them by, if the ship was ever found.

What puzzled investigators was the testimony by the captain of a Canadian ship who passed close to the *Lucky Harvest* a few weeks before she was discovered. He reported that he was on the bridge when his crew brought his attention to a sorry-looking trawler that did not appear to be under its own power. He hailed the ship on the radio but there was no reply, so he altered course to take a closer look and saw the crew on deck, going through the motions as if preparing to drop their fishing nets. As the ship passed alongside, the fishermen looked "as if they had seen a ghost" and stared blankly at the crew of the other vessel. The Canadian captain hailed them again with a loudspeaker, but the men made no reply, nor showed any sign of wanting help. He assumed that they did not know English and that there was nothing more that he could do so he notified the coastguard and continued his course.

FEAR OF HEIGHTS

In the 1930s a terrible fire gripped a large department store in downtown Tokyo, taking several lives. Many workers were trapped in the building, and they scrambled onto the roof to escape the flames and await rescue by the fire services. Firemen arrived quickly and set up a safety net to catch people forced to jump from the roof. After the fire was extinguished, rumors spread that a group of women refused to jump, not because of the height, but because they were wearing kimonos, which are traditionally worn by Japanese women without underwear. In conservative Japan, they were more scared of exposing themselves when they jumped in front of the firemen than they were of the flames engulfing the building. Several of the women perished, and it's said that the story prompted a shift in Japanese fashions towards Western-style clothes.

HEAVY DUTY

Fire crews who were called out for an unusual job in a suburb of Orlando, Florida, were doubly shocked when they realized the scale of the task ahead of them. A morbidly obese woman, weighing in the region of 50 stones, had fallen out of her bed when trying to reach the kitchen. Due to her bulk she was unable to move herself from the floor, and was wedged between the bed and the wall. Horrifyingly, she told the first police officer to arrive on the scene that she thought she had landed on her toddler niece who was playing in the room; she had been watching over the child at the time for her sister, who spent most of her time looking after her bedridden sibling and had left the house to buy more food for her. The firefighters didn't know if she was crazy or lying, but they set to work moving her as fast as possible—a giant job which meant they had to knock a wall down and use a small crane to winch her out of the building. As they fixed the straps around her body and readied the crane, her sister returned home from the store. When she realized what was happening, she began asking where her daughter was; a question nobody dared answer until they heaved her sister off the ground and discovered another much smaller body underneath.

HALLOWEEN HELL

A Japanese student who spoke little English was visiting the United States for the first time, staying with a family in the South. He was invited to a party for his first proper American Halloween experience. Excited, he dressed as John Travolta from *Saturday Night Fever* and travelled to the party with his American friend. The event was in a quiet suburban area they didn't know, and they weren't sure which house the party was in. They knocked on a door covered in Halloween decorations and received no answer but heard a noise coming from the side of the house and looked there for an entrance. Suddenly, a door opened and a middle-aged woman looked out. She seemed scared, and the boys realized that she thought they were burglars. Before the American youth could say, "We're here for the party," the woman screamed and told her husband to get his gun. He burst out of the house, yelling, "Freeze!" and pointing a revolver at the boys. The Japanese boy, not knowing that "freeze" meant "don't move," tried to approach the householder to explain why they were there. Panicking, the man fired off a shot, hitting the student in the chest and killing him instantly. The shooter escaped jail on self-defense charges and later declared that he would never use a gun again.

DEATH BY OVEN

Workers at a factory in Britain were attempting to solve a problem with one of their giant industrial ovens. The machine was shut down and the electrical supply was cut off. A supervisor set to work on a control panel and found the source of the problem, so the electricity was reconnected, the oven doors closed and it was soon back up to temperature. Not long afterwards, staff noticed smoke seeping out from the oven, which was not supposed to happen, as they hadn't put anything inside. It was quickly shut down again and the doors were opened. The factory floor filled with acrid smoke and an awful smell: lying at the front of the oven was a man, burned alive. The worker had walked inside the oven to help solve the technical fault, but none of his colleagues knew he was there. When the problem was resolved, the doors closed automatically as the electricity came back on, trapping him inside with no way of alerting his workmates. He had tried in vain to prise the doors open with a crowbar but the oven was well insulated, and his cries for help were not heard on the noisy factory floor, as the heat rose to almost 300°C. In a further tragic twist, it turned out that the man who had switched the oven back on was engaged to the dead man's daughter.

THE GREAT MOLASSES DISASTER

In January 1919, in Boston, one of the weirdest and most improbable disasters in history occurred. At the Purity Distilling Company, huge amounts of molasses were stored in tanks 50-foot high, ready to be made into rum. One morning one of those tanks broke and 2.3 million gallons of molasses devastated the North End district of the city, with a 15-foot tidal wave of sugar travelling at 35 mph that destroyed everything in its path.

The brown sticky flood brought down buildings and killed 21 people, leaving rescuers to wade through the waist-deep swamp-like sugar to find the survivors, of whom 150 were injured. Several horses were also unable to escape the deluge.

Such was the power of the tasty tsunami that the steel supports of an elevated railway bridge were torn away. Witnesses said that the sound of the tank exploding was like machine gun fire, as the rivets gave way and popped out of the giant structure. The clean-up lasted months, and the area reportedly smelled of molasses for many years.

THE DEMON CORE

A lump of plutonium used to create the nuclear bombs deployed by the Americans in the famous Bikini Atoll nuclear tests claimed the lives of several scientists. In a spooky coincidence, both of the incidents happened on Tuesdays, both the 21st of the month.

In 1945 a young scientist was working on the spherical mass of plutonium at a secret laboratory in New Mexico. He made a mistake in an experiment designed to prepare the substance for use in a bomb, dropping a lump of metal onto the core and causing it to go "supercritical," meaning that the radiation suddenly rose to a dangerous level. By the time he had reversed his error, he had suffered a lethal dose. He died a month later from radiation poisoning. A security guard sitting some distance away developed a fatal cancer some years later.

A few months later another physicist at the same lab, a friend of the one who had already died, was conducting a similar experiment on the same plutonium core, but one that was thought to be even more dangerous. It involved initiating a small nuclear reaction but avoiding the uncontrollable chain reaction that would cause a large-scale nuclear explosion. The physicist was demonstrating the risky technique to several other scientists present. Like his colleague's fatal experiment, it required the utmost concentration, as he relied only on a screwdriver and a very steady hand to make sure that the metal did not get too close to the core and set off a reaction. The scientists called it "tickling the dragon's tail." He had performed the procedure on several occasions before, often in front of observers, and was regarded as something of a daredevil. The famous physicist Enrico Fermi reportedly told him that he would be dead within a year if he continued with the "dragon's tail" experiment.

This time his hand slipped, and the core instantly went supercritical, emitting a blinding flash of blue light. He managed to stop the reaction in less than a second, but by then he had already received a fatal dose of radiation which killed him within a week. Two other scientists present succumbed to radiation-linked diseases many years later. From then on the deadly plutonium sphere was regarded as cursed and dubbed the "demon core."

MICROWAVED MAN

A man who worked on repairing a telecommunications transmitter in Northern Canada was killed after standing too close to the machinery, as he attempted to keep warm during a Christmas Eve shift. It was not the first time the man had got too close to the dish: he had received a warning from officials after dodging a safety barrier and deactivating the alarms on at least one previous occasion. However, he claimed that he got so cold on his night shifts that he didn't have any choice. A company spokesperson explained that transmitter stations were not heated, as the machinery generated its own heat and needed to be kept cool. Clearly, the deceased had planned his risky stunt: he had reportedly smuggled in a six-pack of beer and a folding chair on which he was found the following morning by the next man to come on shift. He was sitting directly in front of the microwave transmitter, still clutching a beer. Judging by the smell, he had been literally cooked. It's possible that a peak in energy caused by extra communications over the Christmas holiday had contributed to his death.

A TRAGIC END

A businessman from London was having problems with his ex-girlfriend, an intelligent but unstable woman from whom he had recently split. One night she turned up at his house in a raging mood, demanding to speak to him. He wouldn't let her through the front door, as he knew what she was like when she was in that state, so he left her banging on the front door and slipped out of the backyard to stay at a friend's house. He didn't see her for the next couple of days, which he thought was odd, but he was relieved to be able to return to his home and get back to work.

A few days later he began to notice a strange smell in the living room, which no amount of cleaning could remove. He realized that something was stuck inside his chimney; luckily, it was summer time so he hadn't tried to light a fire recently. He called out a contractor to sort out the problem, as the smell was unbearable, but the workman couldn't do anything from the roof or from the fireplace, so he started to dismantle the chimney. As he removed the bricks, he was shocked to discover a woman's shoe in the flue, and then he saw the foot still inside. The man's ex-girlfriend had become trapped in the chimney, and she was dead. Police believed that in her distressed state, she had tried to enter the house via the fireplace. She got stuck halfway, and as the businessman was not at home, nobody could help her. At the inquest it was revealed that people living nearby had heard a woman shouting but had dismissed it as noisy neighborhood kids.

A SPECIAL DRESS

Jenny worked two jobs to pay for her college education, and even then money was very tight. After paying for rent, tuition and books, there was only just enough for food. Most of her classmates didn't have the same problems, coming from wealthy backgrounds, so they partied while she worked at a bar in the evenings. One day Jenny received an invitation to a college ball, and as everyone would be there—and she had worked every Friday that term—she decided that this time she would go. There was only one problem: the dress code required something "special." She didn't have anything suitable, and she certainly couldn't afford anything new.

A friend who worked at a vintage clothes shop suggested that Jenny might find something suitably glamorous there at a low price, so she visited and tried out several outfits. She had almost given up when she spotted a beautiful satin dress hidden at the back of the display. It was just what she was looking for, although a little out of her budget, but she had to have it.

On the night of the ball she laid the dress out on her bed with a smile and took her time getting ready. She tried it on again and was sure she looked great. When she took the dress off to shower, she felt a wave of nausea come over her, but it soon passed and she forgot about it. In her excitement she even ordered a cab to take her to the event, which was not something she would normally splash out on.

Jenny arrived at the ball and attracted lots of attention, receiving plenty of compliments and jealous looks from the other girls. When they tried to find out more about the dress, she told them that she had found it at the back of her cupboard. She danced for an hour straight, until she started to feel tired. She sat down to rest, but the nauseous feeling in her stomach returned, and the room began to spin. A boy asked her to dance, but she tripped as she tried to get up and follow him onto the dance floor. He tried to help her, but she made her excuses and left.

She stumbled onto the street and flagged down a cab, no longer caring about the money. The cab driver helped her up the steps to her apartment, and she flopped through the door and collapsed onto her bed. That's how her family found her a week later after she failed to return their phone calls. Her death was a mystery. The post-mortem revealed that she had died from poisoning, but bizarrely the toxic substances were identified as a mix of chemicals commonly used to embalm dead bodies before burial.

The police interviewed everybody at the ball, and the taxi driver, but they were stumped. Then a test carried out on items in her flat revealed that the gown was coated in the same toxic chemicals. They tracked the purchase she had made at the vintage store and discovered that the dress had belonged to a young student who had died in a car crash on the way to a ball only a few weeks previously. She was clothed in the dress for her open-casket funeral, and it was only removed from her body just before she was buried. The chemicals had seeped from the dress into Jenny's pores and slowly killed her.

RESURRECTION MARY

People driving past a certain Chicago cemetery in springtime might get a nasty surprise. Back in the 1930s, a young woman had been at a ballroom nearby with a date for an evening of dancing. The young man had had too much to drink and flounced off in a jealous sulk, leaving the girl to walk home alone, as she couldn't afford the cab fare. As she passed the cemetery, a speeding car left the road and knocked her down. She died a week later in hospital.

Her family buried her in that same cemetery, in the same white dress and dancing shoes that she had been wearing that night. One year later, when prom season began again, drivers reported being flagged down by a mysterious girl in a white dress, only for her to disappear when they stopped. Sightings of the girl, who is known as Resurrection Mary, continue to this day, although they are becoming scarier: people say that when Mary now appears, she is angry, her white dress is spattered with blood and she stands in the middle of the road, trying to make drivers crash their cars.

FIND THE BRIDE

A young couple had decided to get married as soon as they graduated from university. The father of the bride lived in London, in a large, old house with grounds—the perfect wedding venue— and hundreds of guests were invited. The ceremony went off without a hitch and later at the reception, with the drinks flowing, the guests suggested that they could all explore the grand old house with a game of hide-and-seek. The children could join in as well.

The bride was a competitive soul, and seeing as she was the star of the show, she was determined to win the game. She was familiar with the mansion and climbed up to the attic, where she knew there would be a good place to hide. She certainly won the game, because nobody could find her, and eventually the guests went home, assuming that she had gone to bed. However, the groom continued to search for her. Finally, even he got tired of looking and retired to an empty bed in a seriously bad mood, thinking that his new wife was playing a cruel trick—or, even worse, that she had left him on his wedding night. When she didn't turn up in the morning, he called the police, but the trail soon ran cold and they gave up the search, assuming that the bride had got cold feet after the wedding and intentionally disappeared. Eventually, the groom cancelled the honeymoon and tried to move on with his life. The bride's family told him that they had no idea what she was up to either but he assumed that they were lying to him to protect their daughter.

Many years later, when the father of the bride had died, the family home was being cleared out for its sale and the contents auctioned off. The bride's widowed mother clambered up to the attic, which she hadn't seen for decades, to check if there was anything she wanted to keep. She noticed an old locked trunk in the corner; she had not planned to keep it but wondered what junk her husband had hidden inside, so she tried to open it. Eventually, she found a key in a drawer, but when she turned the lock and prised the lid open, she screamed in horror. Inside the trunk was a human skeleton wearing an old wedding dress, ripped and torn after the bride trapped inside had tried to free herself on her wedding night.

HELLISH HOMECOMING

An army officer had recently arrived back at barracks from a secret mission abroad. He had lost several young men on the mission and was faced with the unenviable task of informing their next of kin. He reached the first house on site and knocked on the door to speak to the soldier's girlfriend. There was no reply. He left a message on her answerphone, saying that he would call back later to speak to her, and visited the other families on his grim round of duty. He came back later that evening but again there was no reply. The next morning he visited the next-door neighbors and asked if they knew where the woman was. They replied that they hadn't seen or heard her for a day or two but seemed to remember that she had mentioned something about taking her young children to visit her parents.

After a couple of days the officer still hadn't heard anything; at that point it became clear that she hadn't visited her parents, as they were contacting her friends and asking if they had any information regarding her whereabouts. The officer decided to break into the house to see if she was OK, and when he did, he found her lying dead at the bottom of the stairs, with her neck broken. When he checked the rest of the house, to his horror, he found her two young children dead in the bath. The police believed that the mother was at home, bathing her two young children upstairs, when there was a knock at the door. She tripped on the landing and fell down the stairs, breaking her neck. Tragically, the children eventually drowned. The officer never found out for certain whether it was his knock on the door that she was running to answer.

HOT DOG

A family had gone on vacation and left Grandpa to look after their new home and their pet chihuahua, which they couldn't take with them. The old man was happy to take the dog for a walk every day but struggled around the house, as he wasn't used to all the electric gadgets and couldn't work out which button did what or where all the remote controls were kept. His daughter received a lot of calls from him asking for advice.

One day he rang to ask how to use the oven and, after a confusing ten minutes, she realized that he meant the microwave. Eventually, he got it working and she could hear the beeps in the background. She asked what he was cooking in it, and he replied, "Oh I'm not hungry; I'm just drying the dog out from the rain." She laughed and he put the phone down. A couple of minutes later, she wondered if he was really joking; after all, the chihuahua was certainly small enough to fit in the microwave. She rang back, but it was too late. He couldn't hear the phone ringing over the sound of the fire alarm, as the dog perished, the microwave caught fire and flames gutted the kitchen.

AUNTY SUE

The new parents of a young child were excited about the first vacation they would be taking after several years of penny-pinching. They had arranged for an old family friend of the woman's parents to look after the child, as both sets of grandparents were unavailable. This lady was known as Aunty Sue, and she was excited to see the little one.

The couple waited for Sue to arrive, but she was running very late, and soon it was getting close to the latest they could leave to catch their flight so they phoned to see where she was. It turned out that she had lost track of time and then taken a wrong turn on the highway, but she was "putting her foot down" and expected to arrive in 20 minutes or so.

The couple reasoned that if they waited for her to get there, they would probably miss their flight; they were already cutting it fine. So they secured the baby in the high chair, placed a couple of toys nearby, left food on the side ready for Aunty Sue's arrival and hurried out of the front door. Two weeks later, on their return, they were horrified to find the child still in the kitchen, where he had starved to death. When Aunty Sue had said she was putting her foot down, she had really meant it: she had died on the way to their house after taking a corner too fast and crashing off the road.

POOL PARTY

New Orleans, July 1985. More than 100 local lifeguards were enjoying an annual pool party to mark the end of the season—surely one of the safest places to swim in the city that night, even if they had perhaps sunk a few margaritas. At the end of the party, when the revellers had left the water and the guards on duty were clearing the pool, they found something that their colleagues had failed to notice: a man, fully clothed, drowned at the bottom of the deep end.

The director of the city's swimming pools was distraught: "The lifeguards were really upset. It's a real tragedy. We had all been talking about it. It was the first season without a single drowning incident."

JUST DESERTS

CLOSE BUT NO CIGARS

A lawyer and cigar aficionado from New York couldn't resist forking out $5,000 for a case of rare and expensive Cuban cigars. He saved them for as long as could bear it, but ended up smoking them all in a weekend binge. The next morning he woke up with a guilty conscience, but he thought of a great idea to remedy the situation.

He contacted his insurance company to claim that the cigars had been burned and should be replaced, as his policy covered fire damage. After they had finished laughing, his insurers refused the pay out, but they were up against a Manhattan lawyer, and they lost in court to the tune of $5,000 plus damages, as the judge ruled that the cigars had indeed been lost to fire. Not to be outdone, the company reported the lawyer to the police, and he was arrested on suspicion of arson and insurance fraud—a charge which he had trouble denying. He defended himself in court but soon found himself in jail for a year, with a fine that dwarfed the cost of the cigars.

WARTS AND ALL

A man from a remote country village in western England had a problem with his appearance: an unsightly wart on his hand. He had tried every treatment, but no amount of ointments, potions or doctors could shift the carbuncle. This issue was making him depressed so a friend invited him over to his house to cheer him up. After he had sunk a few beers in front of the fire, his mood lifted and a bright idea came to him when he spotted his mate's old shotgun—a family heirloom that hadn't been fired for as long as anyone could remember—hanging above the mantelpiece. After a couple of pints more for Dutch courage, the man waited until his host had gone to relieve himself, loaded the gun and blasted the stubborn wart, hoping it would be gone forever. When he sobered up, though, he discovered that he had lost three fingers and the use of his right hand, and gained a short spell in prison for firearms offences. The wart had survived unscathed.

TREASURE HUNTER

A British man caused a stink in his hometown after a bizarre experiment left him in hospital with second-degree burns. When authorities dug into the cause, they discovered that he had been conducting a dangerous and decidedly disgusting experiment: he was trying to turn his own feces into gold. He had left the ingredients for his experiment on a heater and waited for the magic to happen, but instead he had started a fire in his block of flats, causing £3,000 worth of damage. Rather than striking gold, he was charged with arson by police and sentenced to three months in jail. As the judge commented, "It was an interesting experiment to fulfil the alchemist's dream, but it wasn't going to succeed."

FUNNY MONEY

A Chinese fisherman had scrimped and saved all the time through his long career at sea to plan for his retirement. When he finally moved onto land, he had to work out what to do with his life savings, because he did not trust his local bank. He decided that it would be easier to dig a hole in the cellar of his house and bury the money there, in a plastic bag, where nobody would think to look for it, and where it would be safe from thieves. He did not give the stash much thought for the next few years, and never told anyone about it—not even his family—but when he heard that the old notes were going out of circulation, and needed to be exchanged for new ones before the deadline, he realized that he had to dig the money up and claim the new bills. When he put his hand in the hole to retrieve the cash, however, he realized that something had got to the money before him: termites had eaten through the bag and torn the banknotes to shreds; they were unrecognisable.

In desperation, he took what was left in the bag to every bank in town, all of which refused to accept the shreds as legal tender. He was distraught, and ready to burn the worthless pile of paper, when a bank clerk joked that they might take the money, but only if he stuck it all back together again. The fisherman let him laugh and took him at his word. It took him several months, and several tubs of glue, but eventually he had pieced together every single bill. He carried the money back to the bank and dumped it triumphantly in front of the same cashier, demanding that he accept it. The cashier did not smile this time, and he wasn't joking when he explained that the deadline for exchanging old notes had passed weeks ago, so the money really had become worthless, in pieces or not. The fisherman had been so engrossed in his repair job that he had forgotten the original reason for taking the cash to the bank.

DANGEROUS CARGO

A man loved to tell this story to his son. He was once a tanker driver transporting jet fuel to the local airport, thousands of litres at a time. One night he was held up on a deserted road by another tanker who had stopped in the middle of the road. Being a friendly sort, the driver got out to see if he could help, and two shady-looking men got out of the cab. They were carrying iron bars and cracked him in the leg before he could get back to his truck. They told him that they had run out of gas and wanted him to pump all of his jet fuel into their truck. He didn't seem to have much of a choice so he limped back to his tanker and let them get on with it. Before they drove off, they filled another container and went to fill up the truck's engine as well. He knew that using jet fuel in a truck engine wasn't a good idea and, being a friendly sort, couldn't help warning them, "I wouldn't do that if I were you." They responded by cracking the bar round his other leg. He knew what was coming so, ignoring the pain in his legs, he crawled behind the safety of his own truck. The thieves sped off down the road, but a minute later the night was lit up by an almighty fireball as the escaping tanker exploded. Sometimes it pays to listen to advice.

IF YOU CAN'T STAND THE HEAT...

Of all the world's dangerous sports, the world championship of sauna-sitting has to be up there with the stupidest. It's exactly what it sounds like: participants compete to outlast each other in a red-hot sauna in which the heat is constantly ratcheted up until all but one person have conceded defeat. The last individual to leave the sauna under their own steam, as it were, is declared the winner. Competitors are allowed to scrape boiling sweat from their faces, but not the rest of their body, and swimming shorts are the only clothing allowed. The sport is particularly popular in Nordic countries, where saunas are part of the national culture.

It goes without saying that competitive sauna-sitting might be dangerous, but one year is seared in the memories of those who followed the sport. It was 2010 and the world championship, held in Finland, was reaching its peak. The heat had risen to an incredible 130°C, or gas mark 2, and eventually just two determined competitors were left in the sauna. The finalists were the home favorite and previous champion, and a challenger from Russia. They had both been training hard, with several hot sessions per day and aerobic training, as the heart works very hard during the competition. The Russian began to display worrying signs of overheating, shaking uncontrollably, and the organizers literally had to pull him out of the human oven, where he collapsed, covered in burns; he never regained consciousness. The Finn was now the only man left but, after seven minutes in the furnace, he was being boiled alive, the skin literally falling off his limbs. He was helped outside and he too collapsed. He spent weeks in hospital recovering from severe burns in an induced coma, but he did eventually recover.

To add insult to injury, his pain had not brought him glory. Since both the Finnish and Russian athletes had to be helped out of the sauna, the title was awarded to the man who finished in third place—another Finn, of course. After much soul-searching by the organizers following the tragedy, it was decided that the championships would never be held again.

HUNTER'S LUCK

Sometimes it helps to put things into perspective. If you think you're having a bad day, consider this tale from Russia. In the macho culture of Siberian hunting and fishing it's common, first thing in the morning, to break into a frozen lake by placing a stick of dynamite in the ice, lighting it and waiting for the hole to appear. If you're lucky, you will bag a few hundred fish at the same time. A pair of keen hunter friends from Siberia had invested in a brand-new pick-up truck, complete with caterpillar tracks on the back wheels, so that they could get anywhere they wanted in the winter. They couldn't really afford it, and were paying by instalments, but they hoped to recoup some of the cost with whatever they caught on hunting trips. They wanted to christen the vehicle with a trip to a remote and inaccessible lake, known to be so deep that instruments couldn't detect the bottom and therefore home to some of the biggest fish in the world, or so the stories went. They loaded up the truck with everything required for an extended trip in the wilderness: their faithful hunting dog, food, a tent, high-powered rifles, fishing gear and, of course, a bundle of high explosives. One of the hunters had decided on this particular trip to save some money by buying cheap explosives from a nearby mine, which had an unusually short fuse, lasting only a few seconds.

The usual practice is to carefully dig the TNT into the ice, walk away and wait; however, with a short fuse, designed to be used in a sophisticated detonation system underground, they couldn't risk planting the stick and running—not on a slippery frozen lake. They would have to chuck the dynamite onto the lake from a distance—more dangerous, sure, but a lot more fun.

After several hours' drive through deep snow, they arrived at the lake, toasty and warm on heated seats, and they didn't particularly fancy trudging on to the frozen lake. Nonetheless, one of the men climbed into the back of the pick-up, where the dynamite was kept in a secure box, and got ready to throw it onto the ice. He told the driver that he needed to get closer to the lake so he could throw the explosives a safe distance away. They got to the edge of the lake, but the dynamite thrower, not being much of an athlete, urged his companion to drive onto the ice. It was easily thick enough to support the weight of even their giant truck.

The hunter lit the fuse and chucked the dynamite out onto the ice, reaching a good distance. Suddenly, the driver shouted loudly out of the window: to their horror the men saw that the dog had leapt out of the truck and was chasing the dynamite, as he usually did with sticks. While the men were waiting for the explosion, the dog deftly picked up his new toy and charged back towards the truck, even though his owners were screaming and firing their rifles to put him off. It didn't work. The dog dropped the dynamite at the driver's door and sped off back onto the ice, ready for someone to throw it again. The hunters escaped by half a second, scrambling onto the shore and watching in horror as the truck was lifted by the explosion before it started to sink into the ice. It soon disappeared beneath the waves.

The men managed to get home, after a few days, and even managed not to shoot the dog in anger. He was eventually forgiven after he saved their lives on a number of occasions by frightening off bears and wolves. The insurance company wouldn't pay out because their policy didn't cover accidental dynamite damage. The truck is still somewhere at the bottom of the deepest lake in Russia.

THE REVENGE

A farmer from Suffolk was driving a tractor, towing a tank of slurry that he had collected to spread on his fields. He had left the house early that morning to make the pick-up and he hadn't had any breakfast. Later that same day, he decided to make an unscheduled stop back at the farm to pick up something to eat; maybe his wife had made something nice that morning, he thought.

As he drove up the lane, he noticed an unfamiliar pick-up truck parked in the yard. It looked brand-new and was spotless. He wasn't expecting any deliveries or visitors so he was understandably curious and entered the house quietly by the back door. There was nobody in the kitchen, but he heard voices from upstairs: a man was talking to his wife, and she sounded very pleased.

The farmer wasn't one to think too much about things; he was a man of action and he didn't like to be made a fool of. He left the house quickly and quietly, and got back into his tractor. He backed the tank up to the unfamiliar pick-up, lifted the hydraulics, stuck the exit pipe through the open window and let a ton of wet manure slop into the brand-new vehicle, laughing to himself. He would have to collect more slurry now, but it was worth it. He drove off, pleased with himself and angry at his wife.

When he returned that evening, his wife calmly told him that she had ordered the pick-up as a surprise for his birthday and that the man she was talking to was the salesperson who was explaining the deal to her.

DEDICATION'S WHAT YOU NEED

It's generally recognized that it's good to be dedicated to your job, but sometimes you can take it too far. A truck mechanic from Michigan was working on a particularly troublesome farm vehicle, which was making a strange noise that could not be located. He asked a colleague to start the engine while he was lying underneath it, so that he could listen out for the source of the problem, but that didn't work. He then had an idea: he instructed his mate to drive the vehicle down the highway, while he hung on underneath, so he could definitely work out the source of the noise.

It was another, more disturbing, sound that the driver heard as he set off down the road, however. When he stopped to take a look under the car, he saw that his friend's clothes had caught on a moving part and his body was literally wrapped around the driveshaft.

THE MISSING MAN

In 1984 a young man named Jake went missing from a small Louisiana town. The former National Guardsman and periodic circus worker was known to skip town on occasion. His family thought that Jake might have gone on the run from the law after having been charged with stealing a car, but he would never be seen alive again. Twenty-seven years later, workers renovating a bank in the town were clearing out the second floor, which for years had been used for storage. When they unblocked a fireplace, they were surprised to find scraps of clothing and what looked like small bones in the hearth. When they looked up the chimney, they found Jake. They didn't know why he had ended up there, but it's thought that he was there of his own accord. Forensic experts believed that he would have died within a few days of becoming jammed in the fireplace.

CACTUS PLUGGING

In 1982 two bored young men from Arizona decided to go for a trip in the desert. They were soon taking potshots with their guns at anything that moved and decided to try the local sport of "cactus plugging," which involved attacking cactus plants, usually by shooting at them and "plugging" them full of bullets, until they collapsed. One of the men chose a 20-foot-high Saguaro specimen thought to be over 100 years old and emptied his gun into the trunk. It remained standing, so he walked up to it and kicked it, causing one of the plant's arms, believed to weigh in the region of a quarter of a ton, to fall off and crush him. He never recovered—a reminder that cactus plugging was not only illegal, as the cacti were protected, but also potentially fatal.

THE STAG

A wannabe hunter was driving back from another failed hunting trip in the woods of Oregon. It was his first trip with his brand-new, and very expensive, hunting rifle, which the sales assistant had promised would help him to bag his first stag. He had been excited about the photo he would show to all his friends, standing triumphant above a vanquished stag with spectacular antlers, just like the pictures his hunter mates had shown him, repeatedly. But not this time.

Then he saw a deer standing in the middle of the road, oblivious to the truck bearing down on him. And it wasn't just any old deer: it was an old stag with a gigantic array of antlers. It bowed its great head towards the truck and pawed the ground like a bull. The hunter seized his chance: instead of stopping, he put his foot to the floor and accelerated the truck into the approaching animal, knocking it out cold. The hunter got out of the cab and nudged the stag. It showed no signs of life. He reversed the truck away from it, got out his camera, set up a tripod and arranged his brand-new rifle across the top of the antlers, making sure that he got their full width in shot. He posed with his foot on the creature's massive head, already imagining how he would show his friends the photo and they would think that he had shot the stag fair and square. He then took a few more photos, hanging his car keys and various other items on the antlers for comedic effect. All of a sudden, though, the animal shifted under his foot and sprang back to life. The hunter didn't have time to react, as the great stag leapt back into the trees, apparently completely unscathed. The man could only watch in dismay as the beast disappeared into the forest, dragging with it his expensive new hunting rifle and the keys to the truck.

ACT FIRST, THINK LATER

A British tabloid newspaper reported the story of a court case involving a respected businessman in a northern town. The jury heard that the man had been working hard on a big deal with a competitor for several weeks, so he had not seen his family as much as he would have liked. This had created tensions between the man and his wife, who did not work, so he had decided to treat her with a new car, a red Mercedes. One day he returned home early from work to surprise her and take her out for an afternoon trip. As he pulled up to his house, he saw that he could not park in the driveway as normal because there was another car in the way: a brand-new Mercedes, but not the one he had ordered; it was the wrong color and the wrong model. He had long suspected that his wife was having an affair while he was at work, and here was the proof. As rage built up inside him, he lined his car up with the Mercedes, reversed back down the road and accelerated hard into the back of the other vehicle. Then he did it again, causing serious damage to both cars. Enraged, he stormed out towards the house, ready to confront his wife. He couldn't find anyone inside so he went upstairs and took a pair of scissors to all his wife's clothes to teach her a lesson.

Then he heard someone calling through the front door. It was his wife, sounding scared, saying that she didn't know who he was or what he wanted, but she had already called the police and they were on their way. The businessman stormed down the stairs and was ready to let rip at her when he saw that she was standing on the lawn, with their daughter, who was home from university. They had been out shopping. He discovered that there had been a mistake at the garage, and the wrong Mercedes had been ordered: he had destroyed his own brand-new car. As the family was deemed to own everything the man had destroyed, he didn't go to prison, escaping with a conviction for only a public order offence—and severe embarrassment.

ALWAYS LEAVE A NOTE

A woman had been out shopping in her local town and was carrying several bags up the high street on her way home. As she stepped onto a pedestrian crossing, she got a shock when, instead of stopping to let her cross the road, a large black saloon shot past her with only inches to spare. She muttered under her breath and continued on her way. At the top of the hill, she sat at the bus stop to wait for the number 44 and saw a large car trying to manoeuvre into a small parking space at the side of the road, with some difficulty. She realized that it was the same rude driver who had almost knocked her down earlier. After successfully parking the car into the gap, a large man wearing sunglasses got out of the vehicle and asked the lady if she could keep an eye on his car while she was waiting for the bus, as he didn't trust the people in that town. She was taken aback by the request, but just smiled in response.

A few minutes later the elderly driver of the SUV that was parked behind the man's car returned to his vehicle. As he started the engine, and prepared to move, the woman realized that he didn't have enough room to extricate his large car from the parking space. She could see what was about to happen, but it wasn't really any of her business. The SUV launched into the rear corner of the parked saloon with a terrible metallic crunch, before the driver panicked and accelerated onto the road, scraping all the paint off one side of the car in the process. The old man got out of the SUV, looking suitably sheepish. "I thought there was enough space!" he exclaimed to the watching woman, shaking his head. "I'll leave a note with my contact details." He went back to his car and returned with a notepad, wrote something and left a page under the windscreen wiper of the damaged vehicle. No sooner had he driven off than the other driver reappeared, his face turning red with rage when he saw the damage. He asked the woman if she had seen the car that had caused it, but she explained that she didn't know much about cars; they all looked the same to her. However, she pointed out, the other driver did leave a note. The angry driver ripped it off the windscreen and read it out loud: "I'm only leaving this note because there is a lady watching me do it, sucker!"

CREEPY STORIES

LIVING DOLLS

Families in a Russian city were disturbed to find that somebody was repeatedly disturbing the graves of their relatives. Over a period of several years, flowers went missing, crosses were broken and bizarre letters were left in the cemetery. The police had few leads but eventually arrested a reclusive middle-aged academic, described as learned—he spoke 13 languages—but eccentric by his neighbors. They searched his apartment and found 30 life-size dolls, dressed in female clothes, displayed all around the dwelling. What's wrong with that, you might ask? A bit strange, but nothing incriminating. He had reportedly been fascinated by graveyards since he was a boy, and he had visited hundreds of cemeteries to get inspiration for his odd creations. When the dolls were examined, however, the disturbing truth was revealed. The professor had dug up human remains from the cemetery and used them to make his creepy companions, mummifying the bodies and dressing them carefully in girls' clothes. He would even hold annual birthday parties for each one. One bereaved relative was told by the professor that he had brought the body in from the cold to keep it warm.

In one of the bizarre notes that he left on the graves, the academic claimed that the bodies were talking to him and told him that they wanted to go for a walk. Relatives had read the notes and could see that the graves had been disturbed, but they never thought that the corpses themselves had actually been tampered with. Surely nobody could be so deranged? After police found the "dolls," the affected graves were opened and all the bodies found to be missing. His neighbors claimed they had never seen any of his creations, but what's harder to believe is that the man's parents, who lived with him in the small flat, did not realize what he was up to, telling police that they just thought it was a harmless hobby.

THE LODGER

You know that feeling you get sometimes, when you sense you're being watched in your own home? That sensation in the back of your head, or visions of what might be behind the door or the shower curtain? Or a presence under your bed or in your wardrobe? Objects that show up in strange places? Sometimes it's not just a figment of your imagination. A Japanese man had been noticing insignificant but odd happenings for several weeks. Food would disappear that he didn't remember eating; he heard strange noises in the night and never found the source; possessions would go missing and then mysteriously turn up again. At first he thought that the individuals responsible for these strange goings-on might be burglars checking to see if there was anything worth stealing, so in order to get to the bottom of the mystery, he rigged up surveillance cameras that sent images to his mobile phone. Then he waited.

The breakthrough came when he saw a woman on camera stealing food from the kitchen. He called the police, but she had disappeared by the time they arrived. Officers expected to find evidence of a burglary, but oddly all of the doors and windows were locked from the inside. Nobody had broken in and nobody had broken out, so how had the woman entered the house? They turned the building upside down and eventually cracked the case: they found her hiding in a cupboard where bedding was stored and realized that she had been living there for quite some time. The woman had moved in, undetected, one year previously, when the owner had left the front door unlocked. She did not steal anything but food, and officers described her as "neat and clean," as she took regular showers in the man's bathroom while he was at work. He took pity on her and did not press charges, but he was left to wonder just how much of his private life this uninvited guest had been observing.

TOO CLOSE FOR COMFORT

A British teenage girl had started to receive messages from a boy who went to her school. It all started off in a friendly manner, and she was flattered. Then the messages became more intense, and the boy declared that he liked to keep watch on her, stating that he wanted to be the first thing she saw when she woke up. She didn't realize that he meant it literally. One night he sent her a text saying, "I'm watching you"; she found it so worrying that she slept in her mother's bedroom to feel safer than she would have done in her ground-floor room. Then just before she fell asleep, another text arrived, "I'm in your house." She dismissed this as a dark joke. The next morning she had forgotten about the boy and returned to her own room.

She was chatting to a friend on the phone when she got the eerie feeling that somebody was watching her. She checked in the wardrobe, and behind the doors and curtains, but there was nobody there—perhaps she was imagining things. Then she noticed that the shoeboxes that usually lay neatly under her bed had been disturbed. When she bent down to put them back, she saw that he really *was* watching her: he had been in her house all night.

THE LICK

A young college student in her first year away from home was given a puppy by her parents to keep her company. They thought she might feel safer with the dog, since she had trouble sleeping at the best of times. As the term progressed, she settled into a daily routine of letting the dog sleep under her bed, where she could feel its presence by putting her hand over the side to be licked. One night she was drifting off to sleep when she heard a drip in the bathroom. She got up to turn the taps off and then returned to bed, feeling the reassuring lick on her fingers. In the silence she again heard the drip. She tried to ignore it but couldn't get to sleep, so she wearily got out of bed again to see what was causing the noise. She tried all the taps and then pulled back the shower curtain to see if that's where the dripping noise was coming from. There was her dog, hung in the shower, its blood dripping onto the floor, and a scrawled note attached to the collar. It said, "Humans can lick as well."

SLEEP TIGHT

A newlywed German couple were driving to their dream honeymoon destination in the south of France. It was a long trip, so they booked a night at a cheap motel that wasn't too far out of their way to break up the journey. They were chatting about the luxurious suite they were expecting at their Riviera hotel when they pulled up at the miserable, drab-looking motel; it had even begun to rain. It wasn't quite a dream start to their honeymoon, but they had spent all their money on the wedding and the luxury hotel that they had booked down on the French coast; also, they had been driving for hours, it was late, they were tired and the manager was friendly enough. The latter proudly led them to the motel's own honeymoon suite, furnished with a large dirty-looking bed. The woman noted that there was an odd smell in the room, even though the window was open. Her husband thought that was the least of the problems with the place but he was too tired to complain, so he closed the window, and they settled down for the night and fell asleep.

In the morning they awoke, and the stench had worsened to the point that it made them retch. They flung open the door and told the manager on duty—not the same man as the previous night—who agreed that the scent was "rather unpleasant," but he seemed to think that they were the ones who had caused the problem and eyed them disapprovingly. He fetched a maid to go over the room while the couple had breakfast. When they returned to collect their belongings, the foul smell had gone, replaced by the pungent odor of bleach and cleaning products. They were packing their bags when the manager hurried into the room with a maid, breathless after running up the stairs. He hadn't expected the couple to still be there and he claimed that he had come to apologize for the poor state of the room. The couple thought that his behavior was suspicious but by that point they just wanted to leave.

When they had gone, the manager breathed a sigh of relief and asked the maid to tip the mattress over, carefully. Underneath was the decomposing body of a man.

NUISANCE CALLER

Lisa was watching TV during one of her regular babysitting jobs, while the child, Barney, was asleep upstairs. She was messaging one of her friends on her phone about the programme she was watching, when a message from an unknown number popped up. "How is your evening going?" it asked. Lisa assumed it was a friend she hadn't added to her contacts list yet, so she replied, "I'm fine. Sorry, who are you exactly? I can't remember!"

"It's someone from your class who likes you."

Lisa now had an idea who it might be: a boy she had given her number to in class.

"It's Jeff right?"

"Yes this is Jeff. How is the babysitting going?"

Lisa didn't think she had told anybody apart from her friends what she was up to that evening. "How did you know I was babysitting?"

"You told me about it, don't you remember?" She didn't, but it was possible that she had said something about it.

"Have you checked on the kid?" he asked. She hadn't for a while, but she lied that she had. It was a weird thing to ask, she thought; could it be that one of her girlfriends was playing a trick on her, as they liked to do? She sent them messages to ask if they were mucking around and they all denied it, which is when she got worried.

"Have you checked on Barney?" came another message. This time she ignored it. Then she heard footsteps on the landing. She slowly made her way to the hallway and looked upstairs; there was nobody there and the child's bedroom door was shut. Maybe Barney had gone to the bathroom. Then the house phone rang. She assumed that Barney's parents were calling, but she heard another voice on the line.

"It's me, Jeff. You didn't answer me—have you checked on the kid? He might be in danger, you know."

This was not Jeff; it was a strange voice she didn't recognize, as if the caller were trying to disguise his identity. Lisa decided to call the police on her mobile, and they told her to stay on the line while they tried to trace the call. Finally, the operator's voice came back on the line, telling her to get out of the house immediately and wait for a police car to arrive. They had traced the call: it was coming from the upstairs extension. Lisa was terrified but she couldn't leave the child upstairs on his own, so she inched her way up the stairs, calling for him, saying that he could come down and watch TV if he wanted. There was no reply, but she daren't go any further. Then a man appeared at the top of the stairs, brandishing a gleaming knife and laughing crazily. "Lisa, you should have checked on the kid," he said.

THE FOREST

A man was taking a walk through a forest on the edge of a small town in Japan. He wanted some fresh air and thought he would explore the area, as he had just moved there, but there was an eerie feeling about the place. The forest was not far from a main road, but there was no sound of traffic, and the tree canopy was so dense that it blocked out the light. He spotted a track leading off the main path and thought he saw something move, perhaps a deer. He approached it and slowly realized what he was looking at: a leg...an arm...and a booted foot. Swinging slowly in the breeze was the body of a man, hanging from a branch above. He froze in terror, until he realized that there was another body next to it, strung up in an identical way, with a terrible expression on his face. As he was running back to town to get help, he tripped on something and to his horror realized it was a bone—a large bone. He didn't hang around to find its owner and hurried instead to the police station. The officers who listened to his story weren't as surprised as he'd expected. They explained that he had wondered into the "suicide forest": a favored place for people who chose to end their lives, which was rumored to be haunted by ancient ghosts of the dead. They didn't even know how many bodies were hidden in the trees, as so many people travelled from all around the country on a one-way trip. The day that the man had chosen for his walk had coincided with the end of the tax year in Japan, known to be the most popular time for people to visit the forest. There was even a sign put up by the local authorities in an effort to persuade people to think of their families and get help: hadn't he seen it? The man replied that he hadn't and was shocked by how casual the officers were about the suicides...Then came the realization that those countless dead bodies were going to be his new neighbors.

DON'T GO INSIDE

A grand old building in a wealthy part of town in Hong Kong had been empty for decades. There had always been rumors that it was going to be turned into a luxury hotel, or pulled down to build new housing, but nothing ever happened and it remained unchanged. There were some who claimed that invading soldiers had used it as a brothel during the war and that many people had died inside. It was registered to a mysterious shell company based on an offshore island, so nobody really knew who owned it. But everybody who had grown up in the town knew that they didn't want to go inside. Police lore recorded that once, when officers had been called to sounds of a disturbance, possibly caused by squatters, a small girl had emerged from the building, brandishing a knife, and attacked the officers as if she were possessed, and then disappeared. The local homeless people wouldn't go anywhere near the place.

A group of girls, who had met at the local school, had heard all the stories and decided to check it out for themselves. They had dared each other to last a night in the mansion and upload anything they found onto the internet. They arrived at the forbidding place in high spirits, laughing and joking about what they might find, as they settled in for the night. It was not until after midnight that one of them asked the others about sounds she kept hearing—couldn't they hear the voices from upstairs? They could.

One of the girls plucked up the courage to go upstairs with a camera, which started to flash uncontrollably as she entered an old bedroom, revealing *something* moving towards her across the floor. She panicked and threw herself out of the window. She survived but was never the same again and ended up in a mental hospital, where she still tried repeatedly to throw herself out of the window. One of the other girls picked up the camera and when the others looked at the images, they screamed in horror, unable to believe what they were seeing. They decided to delete the pictures so that nobody else would ever come across them, and they promised never to talk about that building again.

THE SMITH SISTERS

A boy from Wisconsin called Ben was, like all his friends, addicted to his computer. He would spend every evening playing games online and chatting with his mates. One evening he was up late, way past his bedtime, and everybody else in the house was asleep. He was looking for people to chat to when strange messages started appearing on his screen, claiming to be from a pair of twin sisters, who started chatting about games. Then they said that they were his siblings. He told them that that was impossible—he was an only child—so they explained that they were his much older sisters and that his parents were keeping their existence from him.

Ben was slightly scared, but for some reason he couldn't stop talking to the mysterious pair and stayed up all night messaging back and forth. They told him that they had once lived in his house but he still didn't believe them, even though they had answered tricky questions about the building and about his parents. Chillingly, they claimed that they used to sleep in the very room he was sleeping in. When he asked where they lived now, they were silent for several minutes and then the conversation took a far more sinister turn.

"We don't really live anywhere," they said.

"What do you mean?"

"There's something you don't know. We died fifteen years ago."

"Lol. That's not even funny."

"We aren't joking. We were killed fifteen years ago in the bed behind you right now."

"OK I'm turning my PC off now," he warned. He pretended that he wasn't scared, but he was.

"If you don't believe us, look on top of the wardrobe. We both carved our names on top of it on the day we died."

He clambered onto his bed and stretched up to see the top of the wardrobe. He wiped away the thick dust, which made him sneeze, and could feel scratches in the wood. He pulled himself higher and looked closer. Scrawled in the surface was the note, "J & J—4/5/1992."

"What are your names?" he asked.

In reply, an old newspaper article appeared on his screen. The photograph showed two smiling young girls and the caption, dated May 1992, said that the Smith sisters, Janie and Jackie, were murdered by a suspected intruder in their beds at home in the middle of the night. They were stabbed and hidden in a wardrobe; the killer was never found. The only clues were a series of mysterious messages left on the girls' computer.

"Are you Janine and Jenny?" Ben asked, trying to catch them out.

"Don't be smart. You know who we are."

Ben did not reply to them again. However, he couldn't drag himself away from the screen. The Smith sisters were becoming increasingly angry, complaining about how their parents should never have had more children and about how they had been forgotten. At this point Ben lost his nerve, unplugged his computer from the wall, plugged in his headphones and pulled the bed covers over his head.

In the morning he wondered if it had all been a dream and went downstairs to get some breakfast. There was nobody around, which was odd for a weekend, and nobody responded when he called. He went upstairs to his parents' room, expecting to find them still asleep, but the bed was empty. He looked out of the window to the yard, but there was nobody there. Then he saw a mark on the carpet under the wardrobe, some kind of dark liquid. As he went to open the wardrobe, he froze in fear. He called out again, "Mum...? Dad...?" Then he opened the door and his parents' bodies tumbled out on top of him, covered in blood.

THE PORTRAIT

Online forums and social media were awash with pictures of a painting of a pretty young girl, whose striking bright blue eyes looked out intensely. But most people who shared the image were trying not to look at it. It was said that the painting was a self-portrait that originated in Asia: the last act of a talented but tortured artist who had killed herself not long after her boyfriend had broken off their relationship. People said that the girl's face changed as you looked at it, her soft eyes blackening and becoming crueller and colder. Some people saw the girl morph into pictures of themselves. The caption warned that everyone who had stared at the painting for more than 30 seconds had died the next time they fell asleep—and the same thing would happen to anybody who didn't share the image with everybody on their friends list. Nobody knows if anybody actually died, but certainly a lot of people saw the terrifying painting.

DON'T OPEN THE DOOR

A girl lived with friends in a house share while studying at a university in northern England and was in on her own one Friday night. Her housemates had gone out to a party but she didn't feel like joining them. She had joked that reports of a sex attacker preying on women in the local town were putting her off leaving the house. While reading in the front room, she was scared by a sudden loud banging at the front door, followed by what sounded like scratching, as if someone was trying to get in. Then came a strange gurgling noise and heavy breathing, followed by complete silence. She was petrified and hid upstairs, away from the window. She waited for what seemed like hours and heard no more sounds; reassuring herself that whoever it had been must have given up and gone away, she eventually fell asleep. She was soon woken by some screaming—her housemates had returned from their night out and were making the usual racket. She went downstairs to tell them to keep the noise down and saw that the front door was wide open. Her friends were standing around in the hallway, looking cold and shocked. As she came down the stairs, one asked, "Didn't you hear anything?" Julia was sprawled on the step, with her throat cut. She had returned to the house earlier in the night to collect her purse and been followed by someone. She had been attacked and left to die. The noise at the door was Julia trying to get her housemate's attention.

THE JIGSAW PUZZLE

An elderly lady lived in an old stone cottage in the middle of the moors in Devon. She had been on her own for 20 years, since her husband had died, and had become stubborn and set in her ways. She refused to join the modern world and had no television, and her radio had broken long ago. There was one thing she enjoyed doing after her walks out on the moors: jigsaw puzzles. On her rare trips into town she would buy as many as she could afford, then sit in front of the fire every night until one was completed.

One winter, the weather had been so bad that the bus into town had been unable to get up onto the moors, so the woman eventually ran out of puzzles. She tried to make each one last as long as possible, but she couldn't help finishing them. When she had placed the last piece on the last puzzle, there was nothing else to do but go to bed. As she was mounting the stairs, she heard something fall through the letterbox. It gave her a shock, as it was too late for the post to arrive. She poked her head out of the front door into the cold night, but there was nobody there.

When she went back inside, she found an oblong parcel wrapped in brown paper, which made a noise when she shook it. Curious, she tore off the wrapping. It was a jigsaw puzzle, but there was no picture on the front. She racked her brains as to who might have sent it, but she couldn't think of anyone. As she no longer felt sleepy, she settled down at the kitchen table to work on the puzzle.

It was a tough one, with no picture to refer to, and most of the pieces were dark and unremarkable. She persevered, however, and by the early hours she was getting somewhere. Then something strange began to happen. She realized that the picture emerging in front of her eyes looked just like her very own cottage. At first she thought it was just a coincidence, but with every piece she put in place, the picture became eerier. The ornaments on the mantelpiece, the picture of her husband: it was all too close for comfort. Something told her to stop, to leave the puzzle unfinished, but she kept finding places for the remaining pieces. Then the woman herself started to appear in the picture, sitting at the kitchen table, poring over a jigsaw. She no longer knew if she was dreaming or awake, but still she couldn't stop.

Soon the picture was almost completed: the only hole left was where the window of her cottage should be. Her hands trembled as they hovered over the remaining few pieces, moving as if of their own accord. One by one the pieces found their place, revealing a man in the window, looking straight at her. As she placed the final piece, she saw the knife. The last thing she heard was the sound of the window opening.

THE RED WRISTBAND

You are probably familiar with the bands that hospital patients wear around their wrists, containing their names and other information. In South Korea, they are given a white wristband when they are admitted for treatment and other colors in different situations. For instance, a patient recovering from surgery wears a blue band, whereas a patient ready to be discharged wears green. When a patient dies, they are fitted with a red wristband before they are taken to the mortuary.

One night an overworked young doctor was finally coming to the end of a long shift, finishing up a round of the wards at 3 a.m. He was in the basement and needed to fetch his belongings from the fifth floor. Most of his colleagues had gone home—there was a skeleton staff on the wards—and the patients were asleep. Usually, he would take the stairs but it was quiet and he was tired, so he pressed the button to call the lift. When the doors opened, he saw that there was a very old woman inside. He asked if she needed any help but she replied that she knew where she was going. The lift moved up through the floors, stopping at the third to allow someone else to get in. The doors opened slowly, revealing an old man with a long beard and dressed in a white gown. He started to inch towards the elevator, but the doctor caught sight of him and hurriedly closed the doors, retreating to the back of the lift and leaving the man stranded.

"Didn't you see the man waiting for the lift?" the old woman asked.

"He was wearing a red wristband! I know who wears those," explained the doctor, shaken by what he had seen.

The woman didn't respond.

"You must have seen it too...the red band on his wrist?"

"A red band..." The woman turned towards him, raising her arm. "You mean like this one?"